DATE DUE

APR 0 9 2001		
MAY 1 5 2001		
SEP 1 7 2001		
MAR 2 8 2002		
MAY 3 1 2003		
JUN 23 08		
FEB 17 09		
AG 06 12		
JE 2 4 '13		
MY 0 6 '17		
JA 2 1 '20		
JA 1 7 '23		

Demco, Inc. 38-293

CLASSIC GARDEN DESIGN

CLASSIC GARDEN DESIGN

How to Adapt and Recreate Garden Features of the Past

Rosemary Verey

CONGDON & WEED, INC.

New York

45385

Copyright © 1984 by Rosemary Verey

Library of Congress Cataloguing in Publication Data

Verey, Rosemary.
    Classic Garden Design.

    Bibliography: p.
    Includes index.
    1. Gardens – Design. I. Title
SB472. V45   1984   712'.6   84-9480

ISBN 0–86553–128–5
ISBN 0–312–92096–2 (St. Martin's Press)

Published by Congdon & Weed, Inc.
298 Fifth Avenue, New York, N.Y. 10001

Distributed by St. Martin's Press
175 Fifth Avenue, New York, N.Y.10010

Designed and produced by Breslich & Foss, London

First published in Great Britain 1984 by Viking Penguin Inc., London

Printed in Singapore

First American Edition

CONTENTS

FOR DAVID
who moved a 1770 temple from Fairford Park
thus creating a focus of great happiness in our garden.

Preface

The past can either set alight enthusiasm and imagination, or it can appear distant, irrelevant and obscure. When I began gardening almost a quarter of a century ago, garden visiting and garden history would often make my head swim with hundreds of possibilities for my own garden. At first they seemed hopeless ambitions all of which required endless patience and skills which I knew I did not possess.

One day my husband was left several architectural books, among which was a paper on *The Insane Root*, the mandrake. I discovered that every writer on herbs before Christ to the eighteenth century mentions it, and, knowing little about gardens and gardening then, was astonished to find so many different powers and traditions attributed to a plant.

Through the mysterious mandrake, I became interested in early writers on plants, such as William Turner, who published a herbal in 1551 and Thomas Hill, the author of the first general book on gardening printed in English. Then I began to come across many more celebrated writers: William Lawson, John Evelyn, Humphry Repton, John and Jane Loudon, William Robinson and Gertrude Jekyll. Their books opened up an entirely new approach to gardens for me.

At the same time I gained the greatest pleasure from looking at gardens, from those around Tuscan villas, French chateaux and the early American gardens to Hidcote and Cranborne nearer home. There is so much to be learned from a stroll round any garden, whether a sprawling park or a couple of small borders in front of a cottage. The more you know how to look, where to look and what to look for, the more pleasure you find.

Numerous books have been written on the history of gardens, but they are often both too scholarly and too unspecific for practical gardeners wishing to reconstruct or adapt features that impress them. My intention in writing this book has been to provide an introduction to garden history by bringing the subject alive for gardeners, and to look at the history and design of different parts of the garden in order to show how these can be rich sources of ideas. Adapting and recreating garden features need not be difficult or ambitious. At Barnsley House, we recently decided to improve the vegetable garden. Adapting designs from William Lawson's *The Country Housewife's Garden*, we laid it out with old brick paths. Lawson suggested that the beds should never be more than 5 ft (1.5 m) wide so that 'the weeder women' need not tread on them. This is very sound advice. Then four apple trees were trained as goblets and others as espaliers, both thoughts derived from Versailles.

I hope this book will teach people how to look at any garden they visit with a more inquisitive eye and that it will inspire them to borrow and adapt ideas for their own gardens. Instead of introducing too wide and confusing a range of writers and gardens, I have limited the choice in the interests of clarity, and it is my hope that as the reader progesses through the book, he or she will come to appreciate the influential gardening writers and find it a pleasure to consult them. After all, there is little new in gardening and although we must not neglect the future, the past has a wealth of ideas to offer.

This is not an encyclopaedia of gardening knowledge. There are no rules showing how gardens *must* be made, but there are many examples showing what can be done, and with the aid of Roderick Booth-Jones's drawings, how you might set about them.

It is obviously impossible for one author to be able to do justice, unaided, to every aspect of such a vast subject, and I would like to thank all those people who have generously provided information and advice. Many of them are mentioned in the text and have provided slides for reproduction. I am also grateful to the friends who have taken me to visit gardens in the USA, France and Italy. I wish to give special thanks to Chris Baines, who kindly contributed the essay on 'Practical Meadow Gardening', in the chapter on 'The Wild Garden and Meadow Gardening', thus filling in expert information on a subject on which I have no practical experience.

Rosemary Verey, 30 April 1984

CHAPTER ONE

PATHS, ALLEYS AND WALKS

Paths, alleys and walks are the skeleton of the garden. In the earliest gardens, no doubt, they were simply tracks of flattened grass which developed naturally from favourite or useful routes. A garden with inadequate or poorly placed paths will evolve in the same way, and short cuts will result in damage. The gardener must therefore consider carefully not only the purpose of the path and his choice of material for it, but also whether it suits the overall design of the garden.

Paths play both a decorative and a practical role. They frame the beds into manageable sizes and divide the garden into different areas. They lead on from one section to the next, through gates, under archways, round corners, along vistas. It is easy to forget that 'walks' are exactly what they say they are. Any sort of path is not only a means of getting from A to B, or a feature of the garden to be admired from afar. It is for walking along and for admiring the garden from. In this respect paths should be so laid out that there is never any need to retrace one's steps.

'A marked defect in many French gardens is having too many walks. The way these are wound about in symmetrical twirlings is quite ridiculous. In these cases the garden is made for the walks, not the walks for the garden.'

WILLIAM ROBINSON, 1878.

Straight paths, or those laid out symmetrically, convey a feeling of formality, leading you between mixed or herbaceous borders, through the rose garden, along straight vistas or a pleached lime walk. Always remember that distance is relative, so that a simple pergola or a laburnum walk can be quite short if it fits in with the scale of the garden. Curving paths will take you through the orchard, the wilderness or between island beds. In a tiny garden where the owner wants plenty of incident, winding paths can create an illusion of space, with detailed planting on either side in which every plant is important.

The lay-out of the paths will determine the feeling and style of the whole garden and the material with which they are constructed will help to reflect its character.

Ideas from the Past

ITALIAN, FRENCH AND ENGLISH GARDEN PLANS

Looking back in history we can see how Italian Renaissance gardens were planned as extensions of the house, usually on the same axis as the main doorway into the garden. Those gardens of villas on the hillsides above Florence and in and around Rome have an artistic formality, with wide paths bisecting each other and creating vistas in all directions as well as pleasant places to stroll. The spectator was led around parterres and along terraces by these broad straight paths and so given the opportunity to admire the skill and ingenuity of the gardener.

Gardens such as these were a contained unit, often built on the hillsides above cities, from where there were excellent views of the Italian countryside and pleasant breezes on hot summer days.

This illustration from Thomas Hill's *The Gardener's Labyrinth* (1577) shows the main walk around the edge of the garden and subsidiary paths dividing the beds.

Many of these Italian ideas about garden plans travelled home with King Charles V of France when he returned to his country. In the sixteenth century, gardens of the French châteaux were still inward-looking and confined. The same theme was apparent in gardens of this date in England, which are described by Thomas Hill (died *c.* 1574) who wrote the earliest practical English books on gardening. He knew about the châteaux gardens with their knots and mazes, arbours and alleyways, but scaled them down so that they were suitable for the small English manor houses. In his two books he gives plans for square and rectangular gardens with straight paths, the main walk following the line of the enclosing wall or fence and subsidiary paths dividing the beds for ease of cultivation. He recommended that walks and alleys should be 3 or 4 ft (90 or 120 cm.) broad and said that they served a good purpose the owner might diligently view the prosperity of his herbs and flowers from them and so refresh his dull spirits.

It is often forgotten that the formality and elaborate parterres of the early gardens was essential, for their creators had to compensate for a limited choice of plants.

This is equally true of the enormous sixteenth- and seventeenth-century French gardens—Versailles, the Tuileries, St. Germain-au-Laye and Vaux-le-Vicomte, though we should note that they were created for their total impact rather than as horticultural showcases. The main axis, and hence the central path, stretched into the furthest distance. They were *outward*-looking gardens, giving an impression of undisputed power and dominance, and were meant to be viewed and enjoyed from the house or from a wide terrace; only the nearest parterres were used for walking in.

It is easy to be overcome by the apparent complexity and the huge scale of these gardens, but we should not allow this to prevent us looking at the principles of design which lay behind them. Look, for instance, at how the great gravel walks at Vaux-le-Vicomte are punctuated by the addition of simple geometrical shapes in box and yew. They provide the eye with a scale so that we can measure the size of the garden, and they provide vertical features pinpointing elements of the design so that we do not need to be on the château roof to appreciate them.

English gardens of this time were made on a smaller scale, confined by boundary walls. The seventeenth-century writers who had most influence on our gardens at that date were John Rea and John Worlidge. The former advocates wide gravel paths, 'rolled with a weighty roller'. His book is helpful but compared with John Worlidge his ideas lack imagination and flair. Worlidge wrote for the owners of manor houses with gardens of small acreage. He advocates a circular garden, saying the round is very pleasant and 'the walk that circumdates that garden is not unpleasant, for that you may walk as long as you please always forwards without any short turnings.'

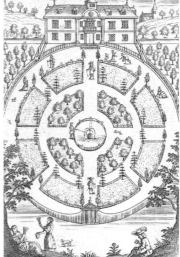

Top: **The parterre and great gravel walks at Vaux-le-Vicomte.** *Bottom*: **Plan for a round garden from** *Systema Horti-culturae* **or** *The Art of Gardening* **(1677) by John Worlidge.**

In his next chapter he covered himself by saying, 'The square is the most perfect and pleasant form that you can lay your garden unto...every walk that is in it being straight. The delight you take in walking in it being much the more as you are less careful; for when you walk in a round or circle, you are more subject to trespass on the borders, without continual thoughts and observations of the ground.'

He has various ideas for material to use. Large gravel walks should have a border on each side adorned with the most select plants and the principal corners marked with flower pots. The best paths for winter and wet weather are those paved with stone and those may have a strip of gravel each side. The overall width he suggests is 4 – 5 ft (90 – 120 cm). Today if stone is too expensive or difficult to obtain then well-textured concrete slabs will weather and in time become almost indistinguishable from stone.

Gravel paths should be edged with brick or turf to prevent the gravel from mixing too readily with the soil each side. If small shells of fish, well pulverized, are added to the gravel it will then not adhere to your shoes in wet weather or after frost. But all in all he considers that grass walks are the most pleasant for they are cool and easy to the feet.

He recognizes the inconvenience and unsightliness of weeds in the path and says that a good way to deal with them is by watering with salt. Perhaps less effective than modern weedkillers, but none the less a very useful way of killing them.

Gradually in England, the fashion for formality gave way to the natural, 'nature was the guide and nature abhors a straight line'. Gardens should be able to look out beyond their bounds, so merging with the countryside. Features in the distance were incorporated into the whole effect, a church spire or ruin could become an interesting visual point, though not aligned at the end of a grand alley and far beyond the bounds of the garden. Garden paths became moulded to the contours, leading along winding ways. Architectural features such as carefully designed steps and terraces were no longer wanted.

A drawing by William Kent of the cascades at Rousham where he created one of the most perfect gardens of the eighteenth-century landscape movement.

Fashions usually change slowly and a strong impetus is needed. During his years as a student at Oxford, Joseph Addison had been greatly influenced by the beauty of the walks beside the River Cherwell—Addison's Walk as it was later to be called—where he enjoyed the natural scenery with winding paths which fitted into the lie of the land. Addison, in his essays or letters written to the *Spectator* between 1712 and 1714, was the first influential writer to criticize formal garden design.

A decade and a half later the popular architect Batty Langley was writing, 'The pleasure of a garden depends on the variety of its parts...that will present new and natural scenes to our view at every step, which regular gardens are incapable of doing. Nor is there anything more shocking than a stiff regular garden.' Langley's book, taken largely from the French, explains at length the lay-outs of parterres and wildernesses. The parterres near the house may have a formal plan, straight canals and avenues not totally banished yet. But as the garden stretches out, the wilderness must have meandering paths and groves planted with evergreens.

Grassy groves and alleys should be planted with standards of holly, yew, bay, laurel, box or phillyreas, surrounded at the bottom with honeysuckles, sweet briars, white jessamines and several sorts of roses. Round these should be a circle of dwarf stock, candytuft, pinks, sweet williams, 'which make no little addition to the beauty of our Plantations'. For serpentine meandering openings should be placed which you 'surprisingly come to', where you may have a pleasant fountain or a garden of fragrant flowers. To add to the pleasures the side of the walks should be intermixed with cherries, plums and apples.

Langley draws attention to the use of false perspective, saying 'that all walks whose lengths are short, and lead away from any point of view, be made narrower at their further ends than at the hither part for by the inclination of their sides, they appear to be of much greater length than they really are.'

This is certainly the transitional period between the formal gardens and the landscape movement of the eighteenth century which reached its height of perfection at Rousham, Stowe and Stourhead.

Pope in his essay in the *Guardian* in 1713 made a vehement attack on the formal garden. He had his own garden at Twickenham, with a grotto, groves and winding paths in the style appropriate to his appreciation of nature. Despite his expressed views, many of his walks were straight and his grove of trees was planted in a quincunx. Theoretical ideas are often hard to put into practice.

Fortunately not every garden in England was destroyed by the landscape influence. In the mid-eighteenth century we have the wonderful 'Gardens of Delight' portrayed by the artist Thomas Robins to remind us of gardens full of horticulture and garden buildings. Amongst many, the delightful picture of Woodside House, Berkshire, shows a variety of styles—the winding paths through the trees, but also a formal lawn in front of the Chinese kiosk.

Today such walks need not be as elaborate as those in Robins' picture. In fact, any area on the edge of a garden can be planted with cherry, plum and apple trees and a pattern of winding grass paths made among them with the lawnmower. But plot the course of these paths beforehand, for even such 'instant' paths need planning. These paths should all have a purpose, for example, a sundial or a statue placed in a secluded corner proves a worthwhile feature and gives 'point' to the path.

One of the next main influences in garden design came with the work of Humphry Repton, the last of the great landscapers. But in his later years he brought back the garden to around the house. He considered that the flower garden should be an object detached and distinct from the general scenery of the place. When describing the flower garden at Valley Field, near the house, he says he would not advocate a meandering walk by the side of a long straight wall, where everything else is artificial. So we have come almost full circle and are once more allowed straight paths—near the house at least.

EARLY AMERICAN GARDENS

The early settlers in America took with them thoughts of their gardens at home, in fact Tudor and Stuart gardens with formal beds and straight paths, usually in square or rectangular plots. This style persisted well into the eighteenth century and the new gardens such as those at Gunston Hall and Stratford and those made at Wiliamsburg were all influenced by the Dutch/English style with neatly clipped 'greens' straight hedges and alleys and box-edged beds.

It is not at all surprising that the new landscape or natural style adopted in England was not accepted. In England the countryside had already been tamed by years of husbandry, while in America each new plantation was surrounded by wild untamed land, to be kept at bay, not emulated. However, two great men, George Washington and Thomas Jefferson, in creating their gardens both bowed in some degree to the new English style.

Thomas Jefferson began his lay-out at Monticello in 1778, the year Whateley's *Observations on Modern Gardening* was published. He was ambassador to France from 1784 – 9 and during those years he visited England and the gardens whose descriptions he had read in Whateley: Stowe, Hagley, the Leasowes and Woburn Farm. This influenced him profoundly. Always an inventor and innovator he combined these new thoughts with the old. At home, at Monticello, the development of his garden covered many years. To match his style of planting, especially using native plants, his paths were curving and serpentine.

George Washington had in his library Batty Langley's *New Principles of Gardening*, a book which explained the transition from formal to informal. By nature Washington was orderly, but his garden became a mixture of the formal and natural. On the east front of his house lay a stretch of 'park land' running down to the Potomac River. His view

Woodside House, Berkshire by Thomas Robins. Note the winding paths either side of the formal lawn.

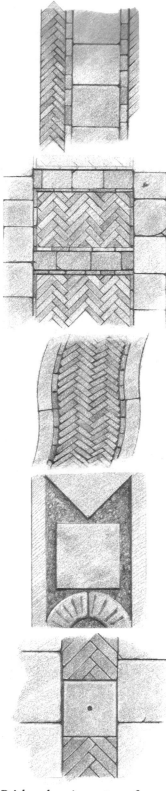

Brick and paving patterns from gardens designed by Gertrude Jekyll and Edwin Lutyens. *From top to bottom:* Orchards, Surrey; Marsh Court, Hampshire; Folly Farm, Berkshire; Amport House, Hampshire; Marsh Court, Hampshire.

of wild unfriendly countryside lay safely the far side of the river.

The west front was a happy combination of symmetry and natural planting. The entrance with twin serpentine roads on each side of his bowling green led towards the mansion. He lined them with native trees, sassafras, crab apples, dogwood, maples, magnolias and tulip trees. In 1914 Charles Sprague Sargent was responsible for replanting these during the restoration of the gardens and now, once again mature, they have a haunting quality of magic as you walk beneath them, picking up a few seeds as a memento of the great George Washington.

On each side the mood changes; there are formal gardens, one for vegetables, the other for flowers in box-edged beds. Here the paths are straight and functional.

VICTORIAN AND EDWARDIAN ENGLAND

In England in the nineteenth century one of the most informative books on garden design was written by Edward Kemp: *How to lay out a garden*—from a quarter of an acre to a hundred acres in extent. He goes into every aspect of lay-out and writes in detail of the formation of walks and paths.

His practical thoughts which are useful to us are that to be perfect walks should be dry, smooth and even, hard and firm; in fact so that you will not slip, trip or get wet feet. A path which is 1 yd (90 cm) wide should be raised about 1 in (2 cm) in the centre, and those of 2 yds (180 cm) about 2 in (5 cm). Wider paths should not be raised any more in the centre or they will lose some of their dignity and effect. Gravel is very variable in colour and quality in different parts of the country, in fact you should see what you are ordering before it arrives. Gravel that has too much lime or clay in it will become dirty in wet weather and break up after frost. Today this gravel would be 'washed', yet with no addition of sand, clay or lime it will never bind. This is all right for drive ways, but for comfort of walking it is necessary to add a 'binder'. Such a mixture will when it is fully set form one of the best possible surfaces for a walk.

The colour of gravel is another point mentioned by Kemp. He considers the best colour is the 'full, deep, reddish yellow so common round London'. White gravels are much too conspicuous and have a cold look. Next he mentions the edging to the walk, and this will affect the character of the garden. Whatever it is, it must be laid with great precision and kept even on each side or otherwise it will look slovenly.

Grass edging will be sure to please: it furnishes the best ground-tint for setting off flowers; it must not be too narrow or it will be difficult to cut, and the edges will be likely to crumble away.

But it is from the writings of Gertrude Jekyll and the gardens designed by her and by Lutyens that we can get a feast of ideas on paving with bricks, stone, cobbles and gravel, to create patterns and contrasting textures. Her books are classics (fortunately now readily available) and should be studied.

Practical Thoughts

Looking back over the old writers we learn many useful points. It is wise to choose your material according to the locality in which you live. Your paths should be slightly convex for good drainage and will look well if they are set off by an edging of another material or with a dwarf or a higher hedge. The path must always suit the character of the garden, straight or winding, wide or narrow, or a mixture of both according to its use and purpose.

LAYING OUT A PATH

As we make an overall plan of our garden, incorporating existing features and creating new ones, our paths will take on their own shape and importance. A functional path, which takes you from your front gate towards the house, should be as direct as possible. It should also be hardwearing, well drained and easy to walk on. This eliminates grass and in some cases gravel. It favours brick, stone, blocks and some of the modern cobblestones.

In a cottage garden the way from the gate to the front door will probably not be too long or broad and will certainly be straight—if it were winding the postman would soon take a short cut. Though functional this must be decorative, an invitation to walk on. Remember the importance of first impressions, for you as well as your visitors. Laid with bricks or stones and a narrow flower border each side planted with low perennials and roses, this will give a clear view from the gate, your eye led enticingly to the front door.

Other paths in constant use will be from your door to the herb garden and the route to your greenhouse. You may enjoy wandering around a herb garden savouring its scents, but imagine how unpleasant it will be on a cold, wet evening to make your way by torch-light along a winding path in order to turn up the greenhouse heating. These are practical points and worth remembering.

In a carefully designed garden, whatever its size and style, formal or informal, you should aim for an easy transition between one section to the next. The pathway should entice you, inviting you to turn the corner to discover what lies beyond, or luring you towards a focal point—whether specimen tree, sundial, urn or arbour. When you reach this and turn again, there should be yet another vista to walk down or a further feature to enjoy. Your garden must never reveal itself at a single glance; you should be able to walk round it experiencing constant feelings of surprise, anticipation and changing mood. The paths must lead you on, becoming an all-important integral part of your garden.

To help you to decide visually on the exact placing of your path, lay a hosepipe or rope path on each side of the position you intend for it. View it from both ends and if necessary leave it there for a day or two to make certain you like it: it is much easier to change your mind now than later. When you have decided the shape of your flower beds, you will often find the position of your paths dictated—for, as Thomas Hill said, 'It is delightful to view the prosperity of your herbs and flowers.' When you have decided on the course of your path, then you must think about the material you will use. Whatever you choose, always make a sound foundation.

A path or walk should entice you, inviting you to turn the corner to discover what lies beyond or luring you towards a focal point as in this Irish garden.

GRAVEL PATHS

For a gravel path dig out to a depth of 5 in (13 cm). Infill with a layer of 2 – 3 in (5 – 7 cm) of small stones for drainage. Allow these to settle and then top up with the required amount of gravel. If you use washed gravel this will just need raking and levelling, if it is gravel mixed with sand then it will need to be rolled and consolidated.

BRICK PATHS

Before you start you must make a careful drawing, preferably on squared paper. Bricks can be laid in so many interesting patterns, especially if you can find them in different colours. You can also combine bricks and concrete slabs or bricks and cobbles in the interest of variety. To make the path, dig out 5 in (13 cm), level the ground, lay a strip of polythene to prevent perennial weeds pushing through, add a covering of 2 – 3 in (5 – 7 cm) sand, level it with a rake and tread it firm. Then bed your bricks into the sand. You will need a line and spirit level to keep the path straight and even.

A simple pattern with bricks and gravel.

PEBBLE PATTERNS

Stone or large pebbles set into concrete make a very effective path. Make some wooden shuttering the width of the path and about 1 yd (90 cm) long. Dig out about 5 in (13 cm), infill with a layer of sand, and then put your shuttering in place. Make sure you have enough stones or pebbles ready to hand, mix enough cement so as almost to fill the shuttering, and carefully tip it in. Now the fun begins. Quickly make an attractive pattern with your pebbles, laying them gently into the cement mixture. They must not sink out of sight, nor must they obtrude too much or they will be uncomfortable to walk on. If you leave the shuttering in place until the right moment of setting occurs, you can remove it without upsetting the pattern. There are endless ideas for patterns. You could write your initials with the pebbles; if the path leads towards your herb garden, you can make your pattern with leaves instead of pebbles. But it is an acquired art to mix the cement and make your patterns whilst it is still pliable.

EDGING

There are many ways of edging paths. Gravel can have brick or stone strips. A 1 ft (30 cm) wide stone strip happily sets off grass paths between twin borders. It is often satisfactory to line the path with lavender, southernwood, box, wall germander or any other plant you can keep into an even shape. Rosemary clips well but you must have an upright- growing variety. Many roses make a wonderful hedge, but choose a thickly growing one such as *Rosa rugosa* or 'Rosa mundi' (now called *R. gallica 'versicolor'*), both of which you can clip.

PERGOLAS

Height is often important in the garden and a pergola is a feature which will give you this instant effect. In hot countries they have always been used as a sheltered place to walk, providing shade from the hot sun, but to me their purpose is decorative, to give support and background to climbing plants and a suitable home for shade-loving plants.

The siting of your pergola is all important, it must have a reason, a purpose, a proper beginning and ending and must certainly lead you somewhere. Build it over an important path, one which you often use. In a small garden I would never choose to put it right down the middle, this would make too much of a division, be too confining. It would be much more appropriate running parallel to one side or else built against the wall of the house or boundary. On the other hand, it would seem to be right and decorative to make an apple tunnel down the centre of your vegetable garden. You could modify this by having a series of arches. A pergola could be used as a division between your flower garden and the vegetables. It may become the way from one area to another, leading you from shade into light. If it is straight then you must create a focal point, an object to walk towards and to draw your eye on. If it is curved then you are creating an element of mystery, for what lies beyond?

Stork pattern made with coloured pebbles at the Villa Gamberaia, Florence.

Pergola incorporating a gazebo in the Pennsylvannia Horticultural Society's garden near Philadelphia.

Opposite: **A simple pergola made of brick pillars, wooden struts and wire for honeysuckle, wisteria, roses or clematis.**

Right: *Rosa* 'Kiftsgate', a vigorous climbing rose ideal for growing over a pergola.

A Renaissance pergola from the *Hypnerotomachia* or *The Strife of Love in a Dream* by Francesco Colonna.

Your decision about what material to use will depend on the situation. Near the house make it architectural and solid in appearance to be in keeping with the mass of the building. Further down the garden a more rustic and casual appearance is appropriate. But if the garden is formal in style it must be architectural and in a cottage garden it may be rustic.

For your pergola near the house you will want square or round pillars built of stone or brick. They should have a plinth or flat stone as a base but if this is lacking then plant some bold-leafed evergreen round the base to give a feeling of solidity; ivy kept clipped to about 8 in (20 cm) or a covering of *bergenia* or *pachysandra*. The height of the pillars in this situation will be related to the architecture of the house, but for comfortable headroom they should be a minimum of 7 ft (210 cm). Make the cross beams of squared oak or treated softwood, one end set into the wall of the house. Timbers of a lighter dimension should run longitudinally and to make extra support for your climbers the entire 'roof' space may be covered with light trellis or timber. The more you cover it the more it develops into a verandah.

This kind of pergola is very effective when built free-standing, but it is only suitable in a formal garden. Constructed professionally it will last for years and will justify the high initial outlay. But half the joy of a garden is making it yourself and a very effective and attractive pergola can be made with far less expense using rustic poles or pressure-treated softwood timber. Recently I bought these latter to construct a trellis fence and was assured by the saw mill owner that they would last for at least thirty years. Sunk two feet into the ground there should be no necessity to cement these into the ground. Stand the post into the hole and fill in round it with small stones ramming these well down and filling every crack with soil. The important thing is to get the base of the post really firmed in. Next put up your cross and side beams. If the structure does not look firm enough at this point then add diagonal braces between uprights and cross bars. It is wise to think about which climbers you intend to use as they will need encouragement and some means of tying

Clematis 'Perle d'Azur', one of
my favourites.

them to your posts unless they are self-clinging like ivy and Virginia creeper. Old wire
netting if you can acquire it will become hardly noticeable if you surround your posts with
it, or you may use the brown plastic-covered netting. The alternative is to put up a series
of vertical wires. The benefit of this preparation is that you will always have a means of
attaching your climbers and will get them shapely at once.

   The moment of choosing your climbers is exciting. The obvious selections are roses,
wisteria and clematis. Decide on the colour for your roses. Do you wish to have a variety
or will you keep to soft pinks and whites? You could have vigorous climbers such as the
species *R. filipes*, 'Kiftsgate' and *R. longicuspis*, which will swiftly reach the top and join
over the middle, and from then on you must keep them in control. For larger flowers which
give beauty and scent around the uprights you could choose the double white Aimée Vibert,
Pink Cécile Brunner, Climbing Iceberg, or Gloire de Dijon. For my clematis I would tend
to keep to the varieties which need hard pruning each early spring. In this way you will
not have the problem of clematis stems becoming too mixed with the rose stems; in fact
it will be possible to keep it all more tidy. Of the large-flowered varieties, *C.* 'Ernest
Markham' or *C.* 'Jackmanii', one of my favourites is *C.* 'Perle d'Azur'. Of the species
and small-flowered varieties my choice would be *C.* 'Huldine', *C.x durandii*, *C. orientalis*
'Bill Mackenzie' and any of the wonderful texensis hybrids especially *C. texensis* 'Étoile
Rose'. In August and September the viticellas are marvellous. They are all delicate and
alluring and a garden without them lacks an important charm.

   For the adventurous gardener there are other climbers to try. Jasminum in variety
and many of the honeysuckles especially *Lonicera splendida*, *L.* 'Dropmore Scarlet' and *L.
tragophylla*. *Solanum crispum* and *S. jasminoides* should occupy a pillar and so should *Passiflora
caerulea* and a trachelospermum. These could all clothe the lower parts of your roses and
add extra interest later in the year. Gardening is all an experiment and if your choice of
plant does not do well, then be bold and change it for another.

*'The climbers I find best for
covering the pergola are Vines,
Jasmine, Aristolochia, Virginia
Creeper, and Wistaria.'*

GERTRUDE JEKYLL.

HEDGES, WALLS AND FENCES

Why do we make a garden? For the answer I quote my friend Anne Leighton of Massachussets, as she expressed her opinion in her book *Early American Gardens*: 'A garden to be a garden must represent a different world, however small, from the real world, a source of comfort in turmoil, of excitement in dullness, security in wildness, companionship in loneliness. Gardening offers a chance for man to regulate at least one aspect of his life, to control his environment and show himself as he wishes to be.' We may take these thoughts further, the Egyptian would not want a garden of raked gravel and sand as in China, it would be too like the desert around him. George Washington when he was making his garden on the Potomac River wished for a formal lay-out in strong contrast to the frightening forest land which lay beyond the river. He wished to keep the unknown and wild at bay. The river was a boundary and he built other barriers in the form of walls, fences and hedges to keep himself and his garden secure. On the other hand, many people today include wild flowers in their gardens because they find so few of them in the hedgerows and meadows where they were taken for granted fifty years ago.

At Thornbury Castle, Gloucestershire in 1520 was 'a goodly gardeyn to walke ynne closed with high walles imbattled'. Further from the castle the orchard was 'inclosed with sawn pall, and without that ditches and quick set heggs'. So there were three different forms of enclosures, high embattled walls, a wooden fence and marking the boundary was the ditch with a hawthorn or quickset hedge. All of these would have kept out roaming animals.

A seventeenth-century garden surrounded by a hedge of roses like the one suggested by John Rea in 1667.

Hedges

Thomas Hill in The Gardener's Labyrinth of 1577 says the 'most commendable inclosure for every garden plot is a quickset hedge, made with the bramble and white thorn'. This is how you should do it: 'Gather in due season of the years, the seedes found in the redde berries of the biggest and highest Briars… ripe seedes of the brambles, the ripe seedes of the white thorne, and to these add both the ripe berries of the gooseberry and Barberrie [berberis] trees. Mix and steepe for a time all the berries and seedes in the bending [binding] meale of tares.' This mixture was then applied to unravelled rope for the winter. In the spring, the rope with the seeds sticking to it was laid in two small furrows, 2 ft (70 cm) and each 1½ in (4 cm) deep, and covered with light earth. This is a splendid idea, for the use of the rope saves both time and trouble in planting a hedge and ensures that it is straight or curved depending on the plan.

In 1667 John Rea suggests making 'a noble hedge of roses.' To do this build a lattice and plant roses on one side of it. Then cut them down and, as the new shoots grow, entwine them into the lattice. I wonder what roses Rea used? By the time the lattice is old the roses will have formed a stout hedge. I have seen lattice covered with ivy in this manner and it looked extremely effective and solid. This is another of Rea's ideas: 'The best hedges for our country are those set with pyracantha and phillyrea; and for lower and in lesser gardens, Celastrus and Alaternus [*Rhamnus alaterna*]…These hedges must be kept narrow, and supported with stakes, rods, or laths on either side, and as they grow cut straight by a line on the top, and even on the sides.' In an old garden I have seen an attractive hedge made with pyracantha with spring-flowering honeysuckle (*Lonicera periclymenum* 'Belgica') entwined through it. This made a firm hedge, sweetly scented and with berries for autumn.

Opposite: Lover attains the Rose from a Flemish manuscript illumination of the *Roman de la Rose c.* 1500. Climbing plants grow up supports to cover the high wall in this medieval garden. The base of the wall forms a turf seat, as well as a bed for the climbing plants which in this story were always roses.

Certain shrubs are conventionally used for hedges and I have written about some of them in the chapter on topiary, because they clip well. These are box, rosemary, bay, hawthorn, holly, *Lonicera nitida*, privet, lavender, hornbeam. Other useful hedges can be made with the evergreens such as cupressus and thuya; many of the berberis would keep out intruders with their vicious spikes but I would not ask anyone to do the unpleasant job of clipping it for me.

Osmanthus delavayi and *Osmarea burkwoodii* make evergreen, scented hedges and as long as they are clipped immediately after flowering they have enough time to make flower buds for next year. *Prunus cerasifera*, the cherry plum, flowers in February and may be kept in shape. The house where I lived in my 'teens had a flowering currant hedge (*Ribes sangineum*) all along the drive and I remember looking forward to the Easter holidays when it would be in flower.

Roses can make a spectacular hedge and every visitor to Kiftsgate Court in June will have vivid memories of the spectacular *Rosa mundi* double hedge. We planted a *Rosa rugosa* hedge several years ago as a wind-break and for three months each year it is a special feature with its scented single flowers followed by masses of large hips.

When you are clipping your hedge do not think that it must be horizontal on the top, it may be castellated or scalloped. In a yew hedge using *Taxus baccata* the upright yew *Taxus b.* 'fastigiata' may be planted at even intervals. This should be allowed to grow taller than the hedge, thus creating green columns. You may do this same thing with hawthorn, holly or hornbeam. A mixed tapestry hedge can be beautiful. At least one yard of the same shrub should be used to prevent a 'spotty' effect. Mix a good proportion of evergreens into it and be conventional in your choice, for if you make a mistake you will ruin the effect of the whole hedge.

In a garden which has expanded into the surrounding fields, I saw an unusual hedge which was largely composed of 'forest trees': oak, ash, and sycamore. It was spring time and these trees, or bushes as they had become through clipping, were coming into leaf and looked beautiful. I would like to plant a hedge like this.

If you are using a hedge as the background for statuary nothing is better than a yew hedge for its colour, texture and solidity. Hedges may often be used to create a false perspective by planting them along a vista with a narrowing path. In this case a statue at the end is appropriate, whereas sometimes a vista should not have a terminal point but should tempt you on to discover what lies beyond.

When you are planning and planting a hedge you must have a clear idea in your mind as to its purpose. It may be an 'architectural' feature which, through its sheer thickness, will have the same effect as a wall. Or it may be a more decorative element, there for its beauty of leaf or flower. It may be the climax of an informal planting of shrubs so forming a boundary where a better defined beech or hornbeam hedge would be too definite.

If you have a bad wind problem in your garden a tall hedge is probably the best solution. The wind will be filtered by it, and thus curbed in its violence and reduced in speed, will cause much less damage. A wall, on the other hand, will cause the wind to smack on to it, rise up and eddy over it. On reaching the other side, your garden side, it will circle back with force and wreak havoc on all your shrubs within the same distance as the height of your wall.

But who would wish to be without a garden wall if they were offered one? It is the most permanent, trouble-free, decorative, useful feature, whether built of stone or brick, or even rendered or plastered. A wall is a clear definition of a boundary, can divide one section of the garden from another. so making gardening in 'rooms' easy, and provides a wonderful place to grow climbers—one of the greatest horticultural delights.

Do not think that just because a shrub is not listed as a climber that it will not benefit from wall protection. Shrubs such as prostanthera (the Australian mint bush), pittosporums, some of the olearias, *Melianthus major*, *Ribes speciosum*, *Buddleia fallowiana* and the vigorous

'Shelter is necessary as a prevention to the bad effects of cold cutting winds. Those points from which the most inclement winds blow should be guarded by trees, and no time should be lost in planting them.'

CHARLES M'INTOSH, 1828.

Escallonia 'Iveyi', to give only a few examples, will flower more profusely with a wall behind them. You can allow some of their branches to come forward and these may be used as 'coathangers' for late-flowering clematis.

Walls

It is not my intention to write about 'how' to build walls, because I believe it is one of the occasions on which you should call in a professional. Badly made walls *always* fall down eventually and usually look clumsily built. However, you should have your own ideas as to how the finished wall will look. In stone country a high garden wall will look best with a flat top of dressed stone. A wall enclosing an informal garden where the fields are part of the vista, may have upright coping stones which stand up tidily like soldiers. Walls inside the garden which are low enough to sit on can be topped with flat stones, unobtrusively cemented for firmness. Walls built around a patio or area near the house can have small pockets left to allow enough soil to establish rock plants such as aubrieta and campanulas. If there is lack of space in this area then, with forethought, seats may be recessed into the wall like window seats in a room.

A wall supporting a small terrace or even the edge of a sunken garden may be amply covered with plants. If a balustrade would look out of place or too grand, plants along the top of the wall will prevent the uncomfortable feeling that you could fall over the edge, otherwise it will be like a deck of a ship without railings.

One of the best and least obvious ways of making a permanent arrangement for training climbers on your wall is to put in a series of vine eyes, spacing them vertically one foot each above the other, then using horizontal wires. These will always be ready to tie the ever-growing stems of your honeysuckles and clematis. Vine eyes are good on a house or brick wall built with mortar joints, but dry stone walls will not hold the vine eyes firm. We have discovered that old 4 in (10 cm) wire-netting is scarcely noticeable when attached to a wall; new netting would shine. The well-used look of the old netting helps to make it blend with the stone. In the summer, I keep a supply of ties in my pocket, ready to fasten any stems before they break in the wind or start off in quite the wrong direction. Prevention is better than cure.

'Take heed of a door or window (yea of a wall) of any man's into your orchard, yea though it be nailed up, or the wall high, for perhaps they will prove theeves.'

WILLIAM LAWSON, 1618.

Fences

The art of making beautiful wooden fences is certainly not in the ascendancy in Britain now, presumably because of the high cost of seasoned timber and because of the labour involved. But in many parts of America one can see how attractive wooden fencing can be, whether using painted or treated wood. Many houses, especially those built of wooden clapboard, would look wrong with brick walls around their gardens. I have often seen wooden fences painted in bright colours to suit the climate and thought how smart they look. At Williamsburg you will see different types and patterns of picket fencing , some looking elegant as a result of their simple design; uprights with arrow shaped tops; a fence based on a trellis pattern; or Chinese Chippendale. A fence should combine well with the architecture of your house and even conform with your neighbour's.

A wooden fence can be a most useful division inside the garden. It may be made quite plain or full of character. If you are using it as a support for plants then do not make it too elaborate. If it is to stand alone then the artistry should go into the design. If it is to be a wind shelter then make it solid. If it is painted white, or a light colour, then it will stand out, bringing it forward; a dark fence will tend to recede.

Recently a friend who had just moved house asked for help to hide what she described as 'awful' larch lap fencing round her new garden. My suggestions to her were to take it down, grow climbers up it, or blank it out with fast-growing shrubs. The first two

'I know a garden set with box will shew very well and will last many years; but it will be three years before the box be grown to perfection; besides, the roots if not cut away on the inside with a keen spade every other year, will run into the beds, and draw from the flowers much of their nourishment; also it must be kept cut three times every year at least. Whereas a garden set with rails, is free from all these inconveniences.'

JOHN REA, 1665.

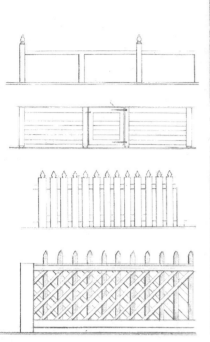

Above: **American gardeners have always made great use of wooden fences. Here examples from a variety of early gardens are shown.**

Above right: **The fence at Mount Vernon in Washington DC.**

thoughts were impossible as the fence belonged to her neighbour. This set me thinking about the question of blocking-off the next door garden and what a pity it is sometimes to do this. Pretty wooden fencing, high and dense enough to keep out or in dogs and children, can become an attractive garden feature instead of merely 'dreadful fencing'. Obviously you would not want the whole of your garden exposed to your neighbour's view so this is an idea which should be treated with discretion.

An amateur carpenter can easily make himself a wooden fence and then enjoy his success. Part of the charm of this lies in the immediate result; no waiting for the hedge to grow.

Always keep your eyes open for iron railings which might get sold as scrap when a property is being demolished, it will probably be of good quality.

A WATTLE FENCE

A final feature feature which you might like to try in your garden is a wattle fence, such as surrounded the medieval enclosed gardens. Simple yet practical, we have probably lost sight of its potential because it is so obvious. In spring when you pollard any willows which you grow for their coloured stems, such as *Salix alba* 'Chermisina', *S.a.* 'Vitellina', *S. daphnoides* and *S. irrorata*, take pieces from the thick ends, cutting them 5 in (12 cm) longer than the intended height of your little wattle fence. Push these firmly 5 in (12 cm) into

An idea for an interwoven hedge, using different species of willow, as described in the text opposite.

the ground at intervals of 14 – 18 in (35 – 45 cm) where you are planning this. Then the fun begins. Weave the willow wands betwixt and between the uprights, tying where need be with raffia or twine. It requires a bit of practice, but very soon you will be asking your friends for all their willow prunings. An amusing artifice to last a year or two, it makes an attractive incident which will protect your seedlings or half-hardy herbs from the wind. For a taller, more permanent structure you will need greater skill and precision. You must allow the wands to take root and then, in the second season, begin to weave the growing stems together, creating what is no longer a fence, but a hedge. If you alternate the different species of willow when planting, it will not only provide a screen of foliage in summer, but a pattern of multi-coloured wood when the leaves have fallen.

Old brick walls are ideal for covering with a variety of climbing plants. An attractive idea is to have a window in the wall, as shown here at Sissinghurst in Kent, to look from one part of the garden to another or into the countryside.

CHAPTER THREE

THE VEGETABLE AND FRUIT GARDEN

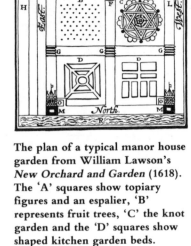

The plan of a typical manor house garden from William Lawson's *New Orchard and Garden* (1618). The 'A' squares show topiary figures and an espalier, 'B' represents fruit trees, 'C' the knot garden and the 'D' squares show shaped kitchen garden beds.

'Carrets well boiled and buttered is a good dish for hungrie or good stomacks...therefore sow carrets in your garden and humbly praise God for them.'

RICHARD GARDINER, 1599.

Modern gardening writers will tell you how to grow more potatoes, and better carrots, sweeter apples or plumper pears. Today it is easy to take so much for granted. We can raise our tender plants from seed early in the year by using propagators and electrically heated soil benches and we can install automatic watering. In winter our greenhouses are kept frost-free with thermostatically controlled heaters, and in summer the windows are opened when necessary by automatic vents so we can go out for the day knowing all is well cared for. However, by reading the old gardening books we can learn a great deal about making our vegetable plots more attractive. That great eighteenth-century writer Joseph Addison understood this well: 'I have always thought a kitchen garden a more pleasant sight than the finest orangery.' Gertrude Jekyll also wrote temptingly, 'I have often thought what a beautiful bit of summer gardening one could do, merrily planted with things usually grown in the kitchen garden only, and filling up spaces with quickly grown flowering plants.'

Old-Fashioned Vegetable Gardens

The first book entirely devoted to vegetable growing was written by Richard Gardiner in 1599. The art of growing vegetables was at a low ebb and he was inspired to write his book after a summer of dearth and had kept many people alive during the 'pinch', or few days before harvest when bread was wanting amongst the poor, by providing them with carrots and cabbages he had grown himself.

In the sixteenth-century—when our knowledge of fruit and vegetable gardening really begins as an art in its own right—vegetable growing was considered less important and was indeed less scientific than fruit growing. In England, this was probably due to one factor—the dissolution of the monasteries. At this time the knowledge accumulated by monks and nuns over centuries was lost, to say nothing of the inevitable disappearance of vegetable and herb seeds. Fruit growing, however, was a different matter. Once a tree was established in the orchard it would continue bearing fruit for many years, providing that necessary pruning instructions were passed on.

WILLIAM LAWSON

If we turn to that charming clergyman William Lawson, we can see how vegetables were considered in relation to the rest of the garden: he had an artistic approach and tells the ladies in his *The Country Housewife's Garden*: 'Herbs are of two sorts and therefore it is meete that we have two Gardens: a garden for flowers and a Kitchin garden...your garden of flowers shall suffer some disgrace, if among them you intermingle Onions, Parsnips.' Lawson suggested that the garden owner, living in a typical manor house should divide his garden into definite areas: his vegetable plot, his knot garden, the quincunx of trees, and his topiary garden.

The kitchen garden was very clearly the responsibility of the housewife at this date and Lawson advised that 'the mistris either to be present herself, or to teach her maids to know herbs from weeds'. In later ages, after the large walled vegetable garden came into fashion at the end of the seventeenth century, the very size of the garden meant that vegetable growing became the responsibility of men.

Today, our vegetable plots are of necessity very much smaller, cared for by one gardener, usually the owner, on summer evenings or at weekends. Do not imagine, therefore, that Lawson is writing for grand gardeners with acres to cultivate: this advice was sound common sense.

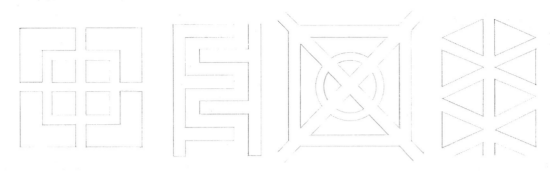

A selection of simple shapes for beds in the vegetable garden, divided so that the beds are easy to weed.

BEDS AND PLANTS

Nowhere is this more apparent than in planning the design. Divide your beds so that 'you may go betwixt to weed', he wrote. Remember this when you are drawing out your design, and make your beds no more than 5 ft (150 cm) wide so you do not have to trample on the soil when you are weeding, sowing and harvesting. The beds can be in simple long strips or, if you are more ambitious, squares can be fitted into 'L' shapes. The paths between these narrow beds need be no more than 18 in (50 cm) wide, in fact just wide enough for you to walk down comfortably by yourself. The paths on which you will use a wheelbarrow should be wider, say 27 in (75 cm): this is the combined width of a 9 in (25 cm) block laid down the centre and two lines of bricks running each side. With the help of squared paper and your own imagination you can devise different designs. Remember that these paths will be there for several years to come so it is worthwhile spending time and thought on the whole project before you start work.

'Be careful not to suffer weedes to run up to seeds: wherefore ply weeding at the first peeping of the spring.'

JOHN EVELYN, 1686.

There are ideas for all sorts of paths in Chapter One on 'Paths, Alleys and Walks', but remember that for the vegetable garden, paths should be constructed with the minimum upkeep in mind. Gravel requires regular weedkilling and is unsatisfactory as it picks up on muddy boots; grass requires mowing. The most practical materials are bricks or blocks. A combination of both, laid in attractive patterns, is probably the ideal for the vegetable patch. Bricks come in a variety of colours and concrete blocks with varying textures, so be sure to go to see them or have samples sent before you embark on a large order. It is important that they will blend with your surroundings.

Brick paths form a pattern of different beds in the vegetable garden at Barnsley House.

SHELTER

The old garden writers were wise in their advice to shelter the vegetable garden from cold wind. A new high wall will usually be economically out of the question, but a fence made with slats nailed to upright posts (2 x 4 in or 5 x 10 cm) and horizontal rails (2 x 2 in or 5 x 5 cm) to form a trellis work is easy to achieve; though inexpensive in material it will filter the blast of the wind. Paint the slats and framework with Cuprinol or a wood-preservative and they will last for years. To save you painting each one, find an old feeding trough or improvise with any pieces of wood you have to hand; line it with a single sheet of polythene so it is liquid-proof, then half fill it with Cuprinol. Put your slats to soak in this for a couple of hours or until they become thoroughly impregnated. When you take them out, stand them upright in a tin to allow the surplus Cuprinol to drain off, as this can be used again. Wear rubber gloves or your hands will get stained. If you have not the time or inclination to make this yourself, you can buy ready-made trellis and attach it to uprights.

There is a large variety of hedging shrubs you could choose. First you must decide whether you want an evergreen or deciduous hedge. Beech, hornbeam, hawthorn are all fast-growing, or you can be much more imaginative and choose a flowering and berrying hedge or one for its scent. If you are short of space the trellis fence is most practical as you can use it in the summer as a support for growing peas and beans or your courgettes (zucchini).

Box-edging round each compartment in old gardens has far more reason for its use than meets the eye. It is amazing how much protection it gives to seedling plants as they come through, and also to newly pricked-out greens. It will inevitably take goodness and moisture from the soil, but this can be remedied by cutting down the roots quite close to the box each spring. A spade or an edging tool will do this very quickly. You may also think that it will take too much time to clip and keep in trim. Today, with the new small electric hand-clippers, you can make a quick and neat job of it. Other plants which are appropriate for edging but probably need more attention are alpine strawberries; these require digging and replanting every other autumn, but they will reward you with an endless supply of fruit from July through until the first frosts. There is a white fruiting variety, quite difficult to come by, which has a delicious and different taste and makes an exciting touch to your bowl of red strawberries.

'All your labours past and to come about an orchard is lost, unless you fence well.'

WILLIAM LAWSON, 1618.

'Chervil is handsome and proper for the edging of Kitchen Garden beds.'

JOHN EVELYN, 1686.

Box-edging provides excellent shelter for young plants and frames the lines of vegetables.

Opposite: **A small square bed in the vegetable garden at Barnsley House in summer—red cabbages alternating with ornamental cabbage, surrounded by lavender.**

A castle garden of the Middle Ages showing small square beds.

Above right: **Japanese onions surrounded by box in a square bed reminiscent of medieval gardens.**

Parsley has to be renewed every spring to be satisfactory and makes an attractive contrast when used round the onion bed. The green and red varieties of salad bowl lettuce make a pretty edge with their curled and fimbricated leaves. They are almost non-bolting especially if you keep picking the leaves.

France has a much stronger tradition of decorative vegetable gardening than England. I would be surprised if it did not have something to do with the fact that the monastic tradition of vegetable gardening continued there for much longer. What the French call their *jardins potagers* often seem to remind one of old manuscript illuminations of monastery gardens.

One thing is certain, France boasts the most beautiful vegetable garden in the world. This can be seen today at the Château de Villandry. It is a modern reconstruction of sixteenth-century gardens based on engravings by du Cerceau. The vegetable garden at Villandry is a revelation. One glance should be enough to set several ideas burning in your head.

Contrasting vegetables in patterned beds in the vegetable garden at the Château de Villandry in France.

DECORATIVE VEGETABLE PLANTING

One of the great joys in having small beds is the many different variations you can make with shapes and colours. You will be surprised how decorative your vegetables can become. Instead of planting runner beans in one long line, use a square bed and sow them diagonally in the shape of a St Andrew's Cross and prick out a good round-headed lettuce in the remaining spaces. In another bed plant alternate red cabbages and Christmas Drumhead; they mature at the same time so your ground will be cleared for a spring sowing. The onion bed will take on a new look if after planting them meticulously in staggered rows you edge the bed with parsley or thyme. The beetroot bed looks more decorative if you grow the golden variety in alternate rows or blocks with the usual red. Swiss chard planted with Ruby chard grown in blocks can make a pattern almost worthy of the flower border. The sun shining through the stems of the Ruby chard is one of the very best colours in the garden. Chicory can look so pretty in the winter, especially the 'Verona' type. Broadcast a mixture of seeds in an area of about 2 sq yds (1.7 sq m) and thin these out when you can see which colours you want to keep to make your pattern.

Seeds of purple brussel sprout are now available and these interplanted with a bright green lettuce make a picture. Use ornamental cabbage and curly kale in random planting where there is a space to fill or where you want to emphasize a corner. Once you start thinking of planting your vegetables in a decorative way, in patterns of colour and texture, you will not only enjoy working in the garden far more but you will also hate to see any bare patches, so you will always be infilling and planting. The result will be more and better crops.

Gertrude Jekyll's ideas for that 'beautiful bit of summer gardening one could do' include using gourds, marrows and runner beans as climbers; rhubarb, globe artichokes and seakale for the beauty of their shape and foliage, not forgetting handsome tufts of horse radish with its deep green leaves. She also suggests that Jerusalem artichokes would make a 9 ft (2.75 m) high foliage screen between the flower gardens and the vegetable patch. This will last for several years, though it is worth adding that it can become extremely dense as the tubers multiply and push out new growth every year.

'There is a great delight in seeing true squares of strawberries, artichokes and great beds of chervil parsley and sorrel, all very even and straight.'

JOHN EVELYN, 1693.

'The enemies of peas are few in number, but great in power. Chopped gorse sown with the seed will prevent the ravages of mice, for the spines will prick their noses.'

SHIRLEY HIBBERD, 1877.

Above: A bed of ornamental cabbage in front of one of Ruby chard at Villandry.

Left: The beautiful Ruby chard.

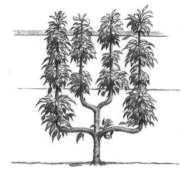

The most commonly used forms of espaliers are the cordons and palmettes. *Above*: A four-armed palmette Verrier, named after a nineteenth-century French gardener Louis Verrier, an elegant form of espalier.

Above right: A double horizontal cordon.

IDEAS TO ADD HEIGHT

Our vegetable garden still lacks a third dimension: height—an essential feature as important in winter as it is in summer. To emphasize the point, think of an allotment field in winter where the only things above ground, apart from a few brussel sprouts and decomposing cabbages, are the bean poles left from last summer and a factory-made wooden shed for tools. Your vegetable garden must be as alluring to walk in in winter as it is in spring and summer.

One way, of doing this is to make some kind of a 'carpenters' work', so popular in France, Holland and England in the sixteenth and seventeenth centuries. Wooden carpenter's work has a totally different quality from the more sophisticated stone and brick garden buildings built as temples, grottoes and follies in the eighteenth century as eye-catchers at the end of long vistas or surprises in bosquets and wildernesses. Their very feeling of transience adds to their charm. Easy and inexpensive to put up, they can be made by home labour in a short time, a weekend perhaps or a few days of holiday. Once there they will immediately add height to your potager, for that is what it is now becoming, no longer a simple vegetable plot but a decorative potager, for use and ornament.

An easy and instant idea for height in the summer is to make simple arches for growing your sweet peas up. The arches should be well placed, probably symmetrically and spanning a pathway. Put single posts 2 x 2 in (5 x 5 cm), 6½ ft (2 m) high each side of a path. Make small holes at 10-in (25-cm) intervals up the posts. Thread wire through the holes and use this to keep 18-in (50-cm)-wide plastic-covered netting firmly attached to the posts. The netting will go up one post, over the top to form the arch, and down the second post. If these arches are used for sweet peas every year it is vital to move the arches. Dig a good-sized hole and fill in with plenty of manure. When the soil has settled it is simple to move your arch to its new position. Paths should always 'go somewhere', and in the same way your arches should have a reason, so site them well—in this case if only to have a good scent as you walk underneath.

If you live in a climate warm enough for Ipomea to flower well for a long while you can make a lovely Morning Glory fence from netting and a few 4 ft (125 cm) posts. This should run from east to west to get the full benefit of the midday sun.

'The introduction of a worthless annual into a garden is a loss comparatively trivial to the introduction of a worthless or bad fruit tree.'

CHARLES M'INTOSH, 1828.

Opposite: Polyanthus flowering before the nut trees come into leaf at Sissinghurst, Kent.

Fruit Trees

An essential part of your garden, and a good way of adding height, is to plant fruit trees. Few people have enough space for a separate orchard, and so to grow them in your vegetable garden is practical as well as decorative.

Start by thinking what shape of tree you want, then consult a specialist nurseryman. It is of the utmost importance that you buy good stock. If you are landed with inferior trees you may not be aware of this for several years, and you will be loath to remove them, feeling you have wasted so many seasons growth.

Apples, pears and plums bend and prune willingly to your requirements and you can choose them according to the space you have available. Bushes have short stems, 18 – 24 in (50 – 60 cm), with branches quite near the ground, convenient to prune and pick. Apples

'I am of Sir William Temple's mind that a good Plum is much better than a bad peach.'

REV. JOHN LAWRENCE, 1714.

grown on semi-dwarfing root stock (MM 106) will eventually make a spread of 10 – 13 ft (3 – 4 m). MM 27 is an even more dwarfing root stock for apples, suitable for growing in tubs and really confined spaces.

Half standards and standards have stems of about 4 ft (1.2 m) and 6 ft (1.8 m) respectively and make a far greater spread. These longer stems need a stronger root stock such as MM 111 and are more suitable for growing in the orchard or on the lawn as a specimen tree. Essentially you must keep the soil immediately round their stems free of vegetation until they are well established and *never* dig round them as this will damage their roots.

Apples, pears, apricots, nectarines, cherries and plums can be bought as fan trees, these will have been especially grown in the nursery with their branches pruned and trained flat, ready to plant on sunny walls and fences. The branches of a fan all radiate from near the base and none should be allowed to go vertically up the wall. Allow a width of 10 ft (3 m) when on a dwarfing stock and 15 ft (4.5 m) on semi-dwarfing.

Cordons make wonderful decorative and productive trees when space is limited. They are much easier than espaliers, the pruning being more straightforward, and when successfully grown they are extremely fruitful. They should be planted 24 – 30 in (60 – 80 cm) apart and trained or laid over at 45 degrees to gain as much fruiting wood as possible within picking reach. Cordons may be planted either as wall trees or free-standing when they make a useful screen between two areas of the garden, perhaps hiding your compost heap or garden shed from view. Where a garden is long and narrow it is logical to keep the vegetables at the far end and the apple or pear cordon screen could be the dividing line between flower and vegetable garden.

Pears do better than apples in a town atmosphere, and in a tiny garden the herb bed could be made square and surrounded by cordon pears. Underplant these with short-stemmed white tulips timed to flower at the same moment as the white pear blossom comes out. Pears Beurre Hardy and Doyenne du Comice cross-pollinate each other and would be a good choice. Make sure the nurseryman sells you well-spurred trees.

At Sissinghurst, a garden of nut trees is underplanted with polyanthus. This makes for a particularly colourful display in spring before the leaves are fully out on the nut trees. It is an idea that could be applied easily to apple and pear trees.

Two-tiered cordons growing at Beaumesnil where the vegetable garden is said to have been laid out by De la Quintinye who was in charge of the Potager du Roi at Versailles. Note the raised beds in the background.

SMALLER FRUIT TREES

Highfield Nurseries at Whitminster, near Gloucester, an enterprising nursery which specializes in fruit trees, has been experimenting with ideas for the owners of small gardens who not only want to have their own fruit but wish everything to have a decorative quality. They sell Victoria plums on Pixy root stock. Instead of pruning the maidens, as is usual, the maiden shoot is bent over after the first summer's growth and the tip is tied back to the base of the stem so forming a smooth loop. In spring when the sap rises it will energize the topmost buds into growth. Fruiting spurs should form on the lower part of the stem and the piece which was tied down will have the least of the sap and will only form leaves. The following summer three or four of the longest shoots at the top will be bent over and tied down and so the process will be repeated. After three summers you will have an original-looking, fruitful yet space-saving small plum tree.

A method of looping Victoria plums on Pixy root stock showing the first, second and third year growth.

APPLE AND PEAR TUNNELS

In a larger garden, where a definite feature is required an apple or pear tunnel is a constant source of pleasure. The frame can be made at home of wood or bought specially designed in plastic-covered metal. The latter may be more expensive, but it will be more satisfactory and long-lasting. The dimensions would have to suit the situation, but a maximum height of 7 ft (2.25 m) at the centre, 6 1/2 ft (2 m) wide and with the top shaped as a semicircle or an ellipse looks right. Each tree must have its own support and a satisfactory distance apart would be 27 – 30 in (70 – 80 cm). Cordons planted as two year old trees on MM 106 should be selected, again with the advice of your nurseryman. The most important point to adhere to is to be patient in allowing the apples to climb slowly up their supports. The rules for pruning must be firmly kept: i.e. always cut the previous year's growth down to a hand's breadth, so leaving six or eight buds only. These will develop into good fruiting spurs for the future. If you leave more you will be left with lengths of trunk with dormant buds and consequently no fruit. Keep the trunk well tied to its support so it will not rock in the wind and so cause root disturbance. An apple tunnel cannot be formed in one season and the final result will depend on correct pruning during the formative years.

'Pruning begin betimes with trees, and do what you list; but if you let them grow great and stubborn, you must do as the tree list.'

WILLIAM LAWSON, 1618.

Closed goblets in the vegetable garden at Barnsley House before their summer pruning. The arbour on the left is well covered with golden hop (*Humulus lupulus*).

CLOSED GOBLETS

An attractive design to develop with your apple trees is to train them in the shape of closed goblets. Choose trees with at least four branches coming from more or less the same point and quite low to the ground. Train these to form the bottom of the goblet, so that each branch is bent first outwards and then curves upwards until it reaches rather less than 6½ft (2 m). If you let them get taller than this pruning becomes difficult. Then turn them inwards to form the lid of the goblet. The training must be very firm in order to make a symmetrical finished article. Wooden stakes could look too bulky. An ideal material is plastic-covered metal painted dark green, using a stake to each of the four branches. The pruning rules apply again. If you are impatient and fail to take off enough of the previous year's growth, you will lose your flowering buds.

THE HERB GARDEN

For thousands of years man has respected herbs as 'plants with a purpose'. He found them in the wild and discovered their qualities and uses. When he dug a plot round his home he introduced those which he found most useful. Today we do the same, and make our herb gardens full of scent and charm with old-fashioned herbs ready to pick for the pot and pot-pourri. The herb garden need not be a grand affair, there may be small patterned beds with neat edgings or the plants can line the pathway jostling for space, cottage garden-style. Whatever we choose it is sure to become a special corner of the garden.

'What is a herb?' asked Alcuin, a Benedictine monk born in AD 735. Charlemagne at whose court he served answered 'It is the friend of physcians and the praise of cooks.' The Concise Oxford English Dictionary tells us in less poetic words that it is a 'plant of which leaves etc. are used for food, medicine, scent, flavour.' In Tudor times the garden for herbs included all the vegetables such as cabbage, carrots and parsnips as well as the herbs for the kitchen and medicine chest. Today our herb gardens range from a few pots of cooking herbs on a patio to extensive herb gardens like those at Hardwick Hall in Derbyshire and the National Herb Garden in Washington DC where you see every possible herb growing. I believe we can allow our imaginations to run on and include all the scented plants we love best, as well as the pot herbs for flavouring. We have learned so much about the wonderful uses of herbs since man began to record the results of his studies, at first in the earliest manuscripts and later in the printed herbals.

Herbs have always been grown for uses. Here they are shown drying, before the leaves and stalks are preserved in labelled jars.

Herbals

We can gain an idea of how important this knowledge of herbs was by tracing the history of a beautiful illuminated manuscript in the Bodleian Library Oxford. It was transcribed into Anglo-Saxon at Bury St. Edmunds in 1120. About 200 years before, it had been copied by the monks of Monte Cassino from a Latin manuscript, which had been translated 500 years before that from the Greek by Apuleius Platonicus.

Another manuscript, probably the herbal with the greatest lasting influence, was *De Materia Medica* ('Concerning Medical Matters') by Dioscorides, a Greek doctor who lived and taught in Rome and was physician to the Roman army in AD 50. Copied and re-copied, it was used extensively until Renaissance times for its advice on useful plants which could be gathered in the wild and then cultivated to be at hand when needed.

Earlier still, in the fourth century BC we find a pupil of Aristotle's, Theophrastus, adding a herbal to his *An Inquiry into Plants* and making use of knowledge brought back by the scientifically trained observers who were travelling with Alexander the Great on his expedition into the vastness of Asia. Before this, there are records of herbs among the Egyptians, who recorded their medicinal uses, the Sumerians, who listed more than 1,000 plants on clay tablets, and as we might expect, the Ancient Chinese.

The first printed English herbals, therefore, stand at the end of a great tradition of learning—despite the fact that William Turner, who wrote the first useful book on herbs (1551 – 68) for the herb-gathering women, claimed that as a student he had been unable to find a book to help him identify herbs accurately. Unfortunately, though full of fascinating plant lore, few herbals of this date add to our knowledge of early garden design. Nonetheless, the illustrations in some are invaluable, and they all have such elegant, delicate language that the personalities of their writers shine through even today.

◀ This painting by Lucas van Valkenborch dating from 1595 shows the variety of plants grown in fifteenth-century gardens. In particular, note the two baskets of herbs in the foreground and the patterned square beds in the background. Many of the flowers in the basket would have been grown for use as well as for decoration.

Early Herb Gardens

From pictures and early manuscript illustrations and from a few printed books by writers such as Thomas Hill, Gervase Markham and John Parkinson we are left with a romantic idea of a herb garden in Tudor times in England. Gardens were enclosed with walls, hedges or fences to keep out straying animals. We can imagine a well or fountain at the centre, and an arbour or a covered alleyway at one side. The raised beds were edged with planks, stones or the shank bones of sheep and a 'fair standing' for the bees was a feature. The pattern for the herb beds was simple and included the root and leaf vegetables. A decorative element was provided by the knot garden, as an exercise in a new Latin grammar book for the Eton and Winchester scholars in 1519 tells us: 'The knotte garden serveth for pleasure, The potte garden for profitte. Let us walk into the knotte garden.' The earlier monastery and castle gardens had been simpler and more utilitarian, with beds in narrow strips or squares, each containing a different herb. This was a very practical idea intended to prevent the herb gatherer muddling the herbs together, and so administering the wrong drug. After the dissolution of the monasteries, however, the country housewife was unable to call on the monks for advice and medicines and had to grow all her own supplies. So as squires and prosperous merchants built themselves manor houses, they set aside space for herb gardens from which their wives could provide plants for the still room, in which they prepared extracts and distillations. A good housewife would have made sure she had all the herbs she required in her garden: for the kitchen, for cures and for sweet-scented concoctions.

This recreated garden at The Cloisters, New York, shows the square and rectangular beds containing herbs so typical of medieval gardens.

et exaltauit cornu populi sui. [] ymn° oibus
sctis ei°:filiis israel populo appropinquati si:
bi. [] antate dno canticuz nouu : laus ei° in ec

Many medieval monastery and castle gardens were divided into narrow strips as shown in this French manuscript illumination. One of the reasons for this design was that it prevented the herb gatherer mixing the herbs up and so administering the wrong drug.

Unchanged throughout the sixteenth and seventeenth centuries, the herb garden was banished, along with the kitchen garden, to corners remote from the house in the first half of the eighteenth century. The new fashion for landscaping demanded an uninterrupted vista. At the same time, it seems that practical husbandry of the herbs and vegetables came to be considered unsuitable for the lady of the house. In fact, women played little part in any form of active gardening in the eighteenth century, only taking up their trowels once more in the early years of Queen Victoria's reign helped, perhaps, by the encouragement of Jane Loudon. The vegetable garden gets scant attention in her *Gardening for Ladies* of 1840, and only the most usual herbs are mentioned, such as parsley, mint and marjoram. These were to be grown and almost lost among the vegetables under the care of the head gardener, so it is understandable that they were little used. It would be unseemly if the cook ran off to the distant vegetable garden for a sprig of parsley, mint or tarragon to flavour her dish, as her artistic fancy took her.

'As for rosemary I lette it runne all over my garden walls, not onlie because my bees love it, but because it is the herb sacred to remembrance and to friendship, whence a sprig of it hath a dumb language.'

SIR THOMAS MORE

Dye plants were an important part of every early American housewife's herb garden. Imported herbs were very expensive, so she sent to Europe for seeds and experimented with tree barks, berries, leaves, lichens and roots. This border shows some of the plants which proved their worth over the years for their lasting colours. They include St. John's Wort, Wood Blue, Woodruff Red and Camomile.

The extensive herb garden at Hardwick Hall, Derbyshire.

'He who sees fennel and gathers it not, is not a man but a devil'.
THE BOOK OF IAGO AB DEWI

As all modern cooks know, to bring out the best flavour herbs must be picked fresh, but added to the pot with discretion, a job and skill more appropriate to the thoughtful housewife than the head gardener and the busy cook. Herbs need a cool hand as well as a cool head. Contemporary cookery books are a sure indication of the use or neglect of herbs in gardens.

By the turn of this century there was a re-kindling of interest in herbs both in England and America. Since then it has increased. Among the reasons for this in England have been the shortage of food during two world wars, the publication by Mrs. Grieve of the best herbal since the days of Gerard, the inspired writings of Eleanor Sinclair Rohde and the famous herb garden created by Vita Sackville West at Sissinghurst. Today, our herb gardens range from a few pots on a patio to the extensive areas planted with them such as those at Hardwick Hall, Derbyshire and the National Herb Garden, Washington D.C. With ever-increasing demand and the established fashion for gardening as both a leisure and a serious pursuit, more and more herb farms are becoming established in both countries. It is one thing to wish to grow a plant and sometimes quite another to find it.

'If we want our herb garden to be really interesting, to be something more and better than a mere adjunct to the kitchen garden, we must be prepared to give it a good measure of personal attention, searching out plants we want'. This advice given seventy years ago by Frances Bardswell in *The Herb Garden* is as true today as it was then. To appreciate the pleasures—aesthetic, gourmet and olfactory—which a herb garden can provide, we must think about it carefully, starting perhaps in a small way and building up our collection as our knowledge and enthusiasm increase.

The Practical Approach

Before starting it is a great help to visit one or two herb gardens to crystallize your ideas. Do you want a formal garden or one planned in cottage garden style? Do you want to keep strictly to culinary and scented herbs or will you mix in others as well? Your decision will depend on how each idea fits most suitably into the general plan of your garden, either with an Elizabethan love of patterns, in a traditional cottage garden style, or a happy compromise.

Whatever your decision there are some essentials to remember. Herbs all love sunshine and most need a well-drained soil, but a few such as mint, lovage, fennel and myrrh will grow in semi-shade. If you are in doubt as to their likes and dislikes think of their natural habitat. Rosemary, lavender and thyme grow on the hot hillsides in Mediterranean countries and their scent is at its very best in those surroundings; given a richer diet they lose some of their piquancy. Herbs which like to keep their roots cool by delving under rocks and stones will grow well in your paving and at the edge of a brick path where

Herb gardens often look their best with the evening light shining on them.

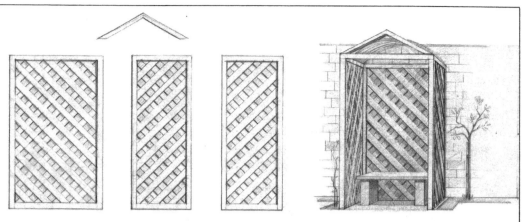

To construct a simple covered arch for a seat from which to survey your herb garden, make three panels from slats and 2 × 2ins (5 × 5cm) wood. The panel for the back should be 4ft (1.25m) wide by about 6½ft (2m) high, and those for the sides 2½ft (750cm) by the same height. At the same time make a small frame for a pediment. Assemble round a simple seat and plant honeysuckle or climbing roses to grow up the sides.

Rosemary growing wild on a wall in Cyprus. Rosemary, lavender and thyme grow naturally on the hot hillsides of Mediterranean countries. Given a richer soil their scent loses some of its strength.

Patterned paving and a central feature such as a sundial will add essential incident to any herb garden.

they will spread luxuriantly. More herbs die through damp roots in winter than by frost. Grey-leafed herbs such as lavender and *Santolina* have a built-in mechanism to help them withstand cold winds and baking sun. This is the covering of fine hairs on their leaves, giving protection against cold in winter and reducing transpiration in summer. It is also the cause of their grey colouring.

SITUATION

Choose a part of the garden which is protected from the worst wind and not under the drip of trees. It should have plenty of sunshine and be near enough to the house to be constantly enjoyed and the herbs frequently gathered. It is good if it can be surrounded on two sides, preferably the north and east. An existing wall, hedge or fence is of course a bonus, but if you have to plant a hedge either *Rosa rugosa* 'Frau Dagmar Hastrup' or *R. rugosa* 'Scabrosa' are ideal and will provide scent in the summer and hips in the autumn.

BEDS AND PATHS

These are interrelated and form the basic pattern. The beds should not be too wide or you will be trampling on your herbs as you pick them and this daily occurrence will do considerable damage to plants and soil. If your soil is heavy and naturally damp you could help the drainage by making raised beds with boards as a surround. This has been a feature of herb gardens since the ninth century and is a curiously neglected idea today. To be practical your paths should be constructed of brick, stone or gravel; on rainy days grass would be damp as you hurry out to pick the parsley. If you are short of space, stepping stones will substitute for paths, but whatever your choice it must have continuity.

A CENTRAL FEATURE TO ADD HEIGHT AND INCIDENT

A fountain or a stone sundial are traditional central features from which your beds can radiate. A statue or an urn raised on a plinth, an old chimney pot with thyme tumbling out of it or a stone pyramid can be attractive. Special 'Ali-Baba' shaped clay pots with openings for herbs or strawberries are available today.

If you wish for a growing feature you could choose a topiary figure in box or holly, or a luxuriant mound of lavender. The importance of this central feature is its permanence. It must look effective throughout the year—an eye-catcher and a point from which your design starts.

SEATS

Find a comfortable place for your seat. The evening is the most likely moment when you will have time to sit out, so make sure you will not be facing the setting sun. It is a romantic idea to watch the sun set in its glowing colours, but your herbs will look better in the evening light if they have the sun shining on to rather than through them. Plant a profusion of aromatic herbs such as rosemary, lavender or the tender *Lippia citriodora* around it. A simple form of arch as would have been used in the sixteenth century could be constructed over the seat, strong enough to support honeysuckle and climbing roses, eglantine, a vine or wild clematis. The simplest method to achieve this is to make three panels with slats and 2 x 2 in (5 x 5 cm) wood. The panel for the back should be about 4 ft (1.25 m) wide and 6½ ft (2 m) high, the side panels at each side slightly narrower. Construct a triangular pediment and roof it in with curving slats. This will be strong enough to last for years.

The medieval 'turf' seats, where lovers were depicted enjoying the seclusion of an enclosed garden, had great charm. They wished to escape from the bustle and noise of the castle hall just as today we sometimes want a quiet place away from it all. If there is a nearby bank then cover this with thymes in different varieties: mingle those with white and purple flowers and the golden-leafed varieties with the silver.

EDGING

The whole point of having an edging to your beds is to give them a framework to emphasise their shape and to help keep a trim look to your herb garden. The best low herbs to use are chives, thyme, parsley, dwarf hyssop, wall germander, winter savory and alpine strawberries. Box, too, is excellent and once established needs little attention except a bi-annual clipping. The herbs will require more attention, division, replacement and seed sowing. It is important to prevent the herbs inside the edging from spilling over and spoiling the framework, so use low herbs next to the edging and the taller floppy ones elsewhere.

Lavender is hard to beat for a low hedge in any of its varieties, except the trailing and Old English which can both become too straggling. It needs a clip every spring and dead heading in the autumn. Rosemary makes a wonderful low hedge. Treat it like any hedging material and clip it from its youth in order to prevent bareness at the base. The clippings will be useful in your pot pourri, as a hair rinse or to help you relax in the bath.

Box hedging makes an excellent framework for even the smallest herb garden and will protect the young plants from wind.

Southernwood, or Old Man (*Artemisia abrotanum*) is another shrubby herb which adapts into an excellent low hedge. It is cheap and easy to establish. In spring put cuttings (9 – 15 in or 25 – 40 cm) of last year's growth into the ground where you want your hedge. Put them 9 in (25 cm) apart in two staggered rows and add a few extra in a corner in case they are needed for infilling. Next and every subsequent spring cut them back to within 4 in (10 cm) of the ground. This is important or they will become hopelessly leggy.

COLOUR IN THE HERB GARDEN

Most culinary herbs are green and are grown for their leaves. When they flower they lose their best flavour, so we tend to keep our mint and chives well clipped. But with space to spare you can introduce enough colour into your herb beds to make them beautiful.

You could create an attractive bed just using the flowers mentioned by William Lawson in *The Country Housewife's Garden*. In his chapter on the 'Husbandry of Herbs' he suggests for the herb garden, 'daffadowndillies', ('they are more for ornament than use'), 'flower-deluce' or iris, ('the roots dried have a sweet smell'), hollyhocks ('the chief use I know is ornament'), mallows ('french or jagged, they are good for the housewife's pot or to break a bunch'), marigolds ('the double marigold, being as big as a little rose, is good for shew, they are pot herbs'), and French poppies ('the seed will make you sleep'). What can we add that William Lawson did not mention? Love-in-the-mist, valerian, catmint, anchusa, bistort, and old-fashioned sweet peas.

Traditional flowers, such as French Marigold, Love-in-the-Mist and Garden Pink shown here, will add a decorative quality to your herb garden and will be in keeping with its old-fashioned air.

SCENT IN THE HERB GARDEN

Scent is as important as flavour to our senses, let us have plenty. Scent may come to you wafting on the air, or it waits for you to approach to take a flower in your hand and 'drink

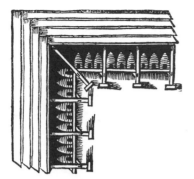

The old books recommend that bee hives should be protected by a permanent shelter. This illustration is from *The Country Housewife's Garden* by William Lawson: 'And though your Hives stand within an hand-breadth the one of another, yet will the Bees know their home...I myself have devised such an house, and I find that it strengthens my Bees much.'

in' its perfume. Roses, honeysuckle and sweet peas are impatient to reveal their scent. Lavender flowers, dwarf iris, buddleias and marigolds will wait for you to approach. Sometimes it is the leaves which hold the secret, then you must squeeze them and enjoy the fragrance on your fingers; scented leaf geraniums, sweet bay, *Lippia citriodora* and marjoram are like this. Put them beside your path to brush against as you pass. Rue has an unpleasant odour to most of us, but it will help to keep flies away from your door, and chives have for centuries been known to keep aphids from apple trees; so will marigolds.

BEES

What better place to keep your bees than in or near the herb garden? Honey was of much greater importance for sweetening food than it is now before the advent of sugar, and every old gardening book has a chapter on bee-keeping. Doubtless all villages and hamlets had their bee-keepers who provided the honey for the neighbourhood.

William Lawson gives two 'good standings' for the bees in his classic design for the garden in 1618. At Packwood House in Warwickshire there are bee-skep niches either side of a seventeenth-century gateway and a niche for the bee-skep in a wall has recently been discovered in the garden at Tudor House in Southampton, England.

Curiously it took a long time to discover the vital importance of the work of bees in cross-pollination and resulting fertilisation. Now their hives are put near bean fields and orchards at flowering time for this reason.

The centre of the herb garden is an ideal place for a bee skep or hive.

Before bamboo canes were in common use in our gardens, supports were made for plants in beds, pots and tubs with woven willow wands. The pollarded willow provided the pliable material for making this interlacing thread, and was a decorative way of keeping the gilliflowers (carnations) and lilies upright. We have tried this at Barnsley House and found it to be an admirable method. The most practical way is to start with the diagonals, making these the ultimate height you will require. Stick each end firmly in the edge of your container, then with slightly shorter wands put another each side of the diagonals, weaving them as you do so. Then add two more each side and weave them in place. You must keep the shape like the top half of an egg.

PLANTS TO ADD HEIGHT

Nature is very obliging and many plants lend themselves to shaping, as gardeners knew so well in the early days. In fact until influential critics like Alexander Pope and Joseph Addison began to ridicule the use of topiary and clipped greens, examples would have been in every garden in the land.

Rosemary, box, holly and *Phillyrea* were all clipped into figures and shapes. Yew was not treated as a topiary subject until later owing to its association with death. Honeysuckle was allowed to grow into standards with 'lollipop' heads, and roses were trained in various ways. All these can be used as features to add height, a third dimension for the pattern

Part of the herb garden at Barnsley House, Gloucestershire. Group naturally tall herbs such as fennel, lovage and rosemary together. Since many herbs are low plants, this will add a third dimension.

of your herb garden. They are like exclamation marks and attract the eye. These features should be free-standing so they may be viewed from all sides, but the naturally tall herbs such as fennel, lovage, angelica and hollyhocks should be grouped together, either in the centre of a square or against a wall or hedge which will protect them from the wind.

POTS FOR THE PATIO

The smallest herb garden can be just a few herbs growing in containers standing on a patio or outside your kitchen door. Only the most useful culinary herbs should be chosen for this, with a few flowering plants if space allows. A large tub or pot could have rosemary as a central feature. Select a variety which has a naturally upright habit of growth and surround this with low perennial herbs, such as clumps of chives, thyme and marjoram. If you buy them as young plants in containers you will have an instant herb garden. Note that it is better to keep your perennials and annuals in separate containers for ease of cultivation. Your container with annuals can then have a change of soil and a new design each spring. If growing them from seed, you must plan ahead to have young plants all ready in the spring. Parsley is essential in the kitchen and you could surround your tub with this, then infill with basil, sweet marjoram, dill and chervil.

Keep your mint by itself, its roots are too invasive to be good neighbours. When you buy mint do taste or at least squeeze a leaf and smell it. Of all herbs it is one of the easiest to grow, but sometimes does not have that true mint flavour we associate with freshly cooked new potatoes.

A bay tree in a pot will add distinction to your miniature herb garden, and if you wish for colour sow a few nasturtium seeds around the edge of the container; grey rue would also be a fine contrast to the bay. If you decide on tomato plants then pot marigolds flowering around them will help keep away aphids and white fly.

Remember that your herb tubs must have as much sunshine as possible, regular watering and feeding.

A SMALL INFORMAL HERB GARDEN

Select a south-east to south-west facing site in the shelter of your house, or a corner by the garage or greenhouse. Suppose it is a bed 4–5 yds (3.5–4.5 m) long and 4 ft (1.25 m) wide. You want this to be attractive as well as useful so plan your planting carefully.

First make a list of herbs which you will need in your cooking. A good selection for this sized bed would be bay, sage and rosemary for evergreen height. Place them in that order at equal distances down the centre of your bed. Fennel and lovage are tall perennials and should go at the back, staggered behind your three shrubs. Balm and mint are both spreaders so put these at each back corner. In one front corner put chives and in the other a variety of different thymes. A sizeable patch of golden marjoram will occupy the front in the centre. Tuck some French (not Russian) tarragon between the bay and the sage.

Your most useful annuals are parsley, basil and chervil. Sow parsley and basil seed in trays indoors and when large enough to transplant outside, put the parsley round the rosemary and the basil each side of the marjoram. Scatter chervil seed around the lovage and fennel. You can of course adapt this idea using other herbs to suit your taste.

If you feel more ambitious make a square herb garden divided into four smaller squares, four or eight triangles, or with a surrounding bed and small squares inside. The paths should be paved with bricks and the regularity of your beds needs to be outlined in box or a mixture of box for some and dwarf lavender, hyssop or any of the other edging plants for others. The beauty of this type of herb garden will be in its pattern as well as its planting.

Each bed could have a tall shrub in the centre: myrtle, a standard rose or honeysuckle with herbs grading down in height towards the edges. The beds could alternate with green and grey shrubs, and the tallest be kept together. There are endless possibilities and luckily, if you make a mistake, all herbs are easy to transplant.

'This for a general rule note, that all flowres, hearbes and rootes, ought carefully to be gathered in a drie faire season, and not in clowdie, mistie, nor rainy weather'.

DIDYMUS MOUNTAIN 1577

'I judge that the flowers of Lavender quilted in a cap and dayly worne are good for all diseases of the head that come of a cold cause and that they comfort the braine very well.'

WILLIAM TURNER 1551

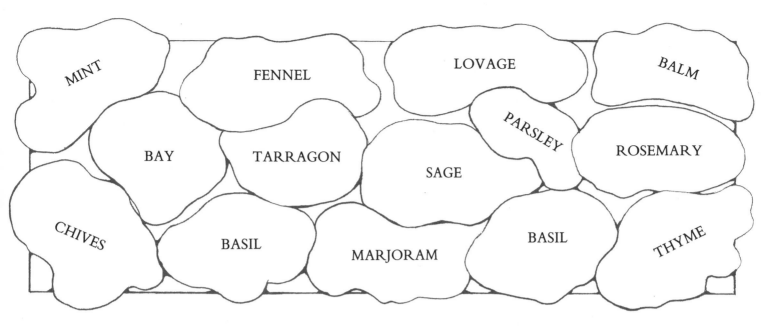

MINT · FENNEL · LOVAGE · BALM · BAY · TARRAGON · PARSLEY · ROSEMARY · SAGE · CHIVES · BASIL · MARJORAM · BASIL · THYME

If you have a cottage garden and are herb and scent mad, you will want your herb garden immediately outside the door from your main sitting-room. In your design treat the door as the point from which the garden is viewed. You will want a small paved area where you can sit. Make this a semicircle with paths radiating like an eighteenth-century *patte d'oie* in miniature. The beds must be narrow and so must the paths, which could be stepping stones in this case.

A herb garden is like a stage set, with low plants in front gradually building up in height towards the back. A back drop of trees is ideal to keep in the warmth. To left and right taller evergreens represent the wings of the stage. The herb grower is suddenly both actor and audience.

Planting plan for a small informal herb garden measuring 4 × 12ft (1.25 × 3.5m).

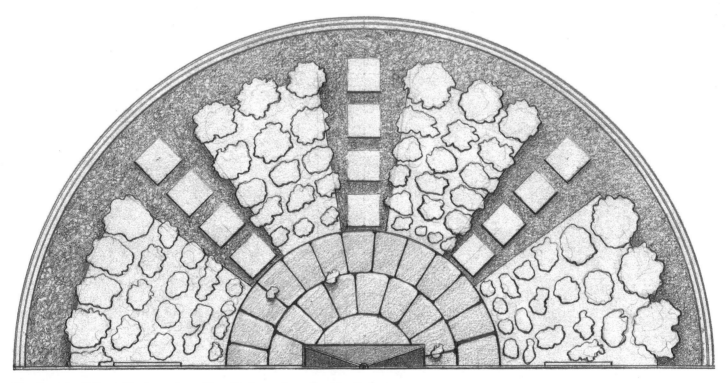

Plan for a small formal herb garden with radiating paths at the side of a house.

CHAPTER FIVE

KNOTS

A purse in the Bodleian Museum, Oxford, embroidered for Queen Elizabeth I with a simple knot pattern.

There are few aspects of gardening so close to pure design as garden knots. Old-fashioned, certainly, they summon up the ghosts of the Elizabethan and Jacobean world, yielding as much pleasure as can be gained from planning them as from planting them.

From early times, knot designs have been used as decorative patterns in many forms of art. The geometrical crosses made up of interlacing threads which adorn Celtic ornaments are knots. So are the intricate designs of Oriental carpets which may, indeed, have provided the source of inspiration for the use of knot patterns in gardens. Rugs began to be imported into Italy in the mid-fifteenth century and a short while later into the Netherlands. We even find them in paintings of the same date.

The heyday of knots was in the sixteenth century. They appeared in embroidery, bookbinding, as strapwork on wooden panelling and as decorative plasterwork. Sometimes a boss in the centre of a ceiling took the form of an interlaced knot—a joke or 'conceit' to assure the onlooker that the ceiling was secure. As a result, we should not be surprised to find that knot gardens became an important decorative feature of western European gardens in the sixteenth and early seventeenth centuries. They appear, quite suddenly, as one of the major innovations of the time, and then disappear. However, we still have patterns of knot designs in the Tudor and Stuart gardening books.

The First Knot Gardens

The first knot illustrations and descriptions of knots in a garden appear in a poem, *Hypnerotomachia* or *The Strife of Love in a Dream*, by the Dominican monk Francesco Colonna, written in 1467 but only published over thirty years later. An imaginary garden is described, with clipped hedges made of myrtle and cypress, and knots with patterns drawn out with marjoram, rue, thyme and lavender cotton—much the same plants in fact that one would advise anyone to use in their knot garden today. The patterns, Colonna says, resemble *tapeti*, or carpets. Most dreams have a basis in reality, so it is natural to assume that Colonna's dream garden was influenced by an existing garden known to him.

Some time before 1517 George, Cardinal d'Amboise, one of Louis XII's chief councillors, made a bed in his garden at Gaillon in which the arms of France were represented in herbs and low-growing flowers; a tribute to his king.

In the same century, Giovanvittorio Soderini, the author of an agricultural treatise, mentions coats of arms, clocks and even human figures made with sweet-smelling herbs. There was a constant trade in ideas and designs, and all these were later used in France and England.

In England the earliest references to knot gardens come from two very diverse sources: a school book (see Chapter Four, 'The Herb Garden') and household accounts. The latter record that in 1520 at Thornbury Castle, Gloucestershire, Edward Stafford, Duke of Buckingham, paid John Wynde the sum of three shillings and fourpence 'for diligence in making knots'. Other estate accounts show that Buckingham's brother-in-law Henry Percy paid a labourer 'for setting of herbs and clipping of knottes'.

Buckingham's heraldic badge was a knot, Percy's a double manacle, both of which could easily be converted into decorative knot patterns in the garden, as we shall see.

While Buckingham was busy at Thornbury, Wolsey was starting to build his palace at Hampton Court, where according to George Cavendish he made 'knottes so enknotted it cannot be exprest'. Wolsey had his knotted beds adjoining his privy rooms, so that he

Opposite: The knot garden at Hampton Court, London as it is today. In the sixteenth century Cardinal Wolsey made knots here that were 'so enknotted it cannot be exprest'.

Above: A knot from Thomas
Hill's The Gardener's Labyrinth
(1577) which could be an
adaptation of the Duke of
Buckingham's heraldic badge.

Right: Making a knot.
1. Make a square bed of the size
required.
2. Find the centre of the square
by stretching strings across it
from corner to corner. Place a
peg at this centre point. Attach a
piece of string to a bottle filled
with sand. Stand the bottle at the
edge of the bed half way along
one side and then tie the string to
the central peg. Then, using this
primitive compass, make a circle
of sand.
3. Next, place a peg outside the
bed halfway between two corners
and make a semi-circle. Repeat at
each side.
4. Now, place the pegs inside the
bed and stretch string between
them. Pour more sand along the
line of the string. Finally, plant
with different species of herb 3-4
in (7-10cm) apart. For example,
thyme for the square, hyssop for
the semi-circles and marjoram for
the circle. Your knot may be
planted using only box. Fill the
spaces between with coloured
gravel.

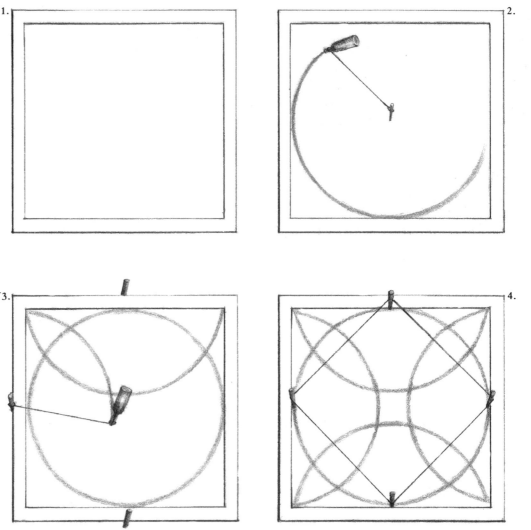

could look down on them from his windows and enjoy their pattern. In all probability many such knot gardens were being made in England in the early sixteenth century. In France, where François I was making his garden at Fontainebleau and Catherine de Medici one at Monceaux, we have a clear picture of how gardens were laid out from a volume of engravings entitled *Les Plus Excellents Bastiments de France*. Mazes and knots were among the features used in gardens that were generally created inside existing castle walls, in contrast with Italy where house and garden were conceived as a unit.

In *The Profitable Arte of Gardening* (1563), Thomas Hill gives an elaborate design for a knot far more suitable for embroidery than herbs, but called 'A Proper Knot for a Garden, where is spare rooms enough, the which may be set either with Thyme or Issope, at the discretion of the gardener'. In his second book, *The Gardener's Labyrinth*, there are two designs for knots. The one based on a circle and four semi-circles is an elaboration of the Duke of Buckingham's knot with a square in the centre to hold the pattern together. This and the second design, which evolved from interlacing figures of eight or, one could say, double manacles (Percy's badge), would both look attractive carried out in thyme and hyssop, or marjoram and thyme.

Hill's books were written for the numerous small country manor houses built during the second half of the sixteenth century. Given the current love of detail and design and the desire to create interesting garden features, it is natural that knot gardens became fashionable.

It is surprising, however, that Hill's books pre-date the most influential French work on how to lay out and make a knot garden. This appeared in the 1583 and subsequent editions of *L' Agriculture et Maison Rustique* by Charles Estienne and Jean Liebault. Gervase Markham's translation of the 1616 tells us a great deal more about knots. In fact, all that we really need to know today.

Designing a Knot Garden

When you are laying out a knot it is as well to follow Gervase Markham's advice. First draw your design on paper, then sketch in the diagonals and a grid running both ways. Next, measure your knot and peg out the corners on the ground. Get many measures of small cord, reels, dibbles and rods the thickness of your thumb. Set out the cord to represent the grid you have drawn on your design, and 'draw' the design on the ground using dry sand or lime.

For 'roundwork' you must have an instrument commonly called a bilboquet, which is a piece of string with a peg one end and knots at intervals of 8 in (20 cm) into which another peg can be inserted. This can then be used as a compass to 'draw' your circle or roundwork upon the ground.

The nature of the proportions will, Markham says, 'Depend upon the spirit of the gardener and also the pleasure of the master'. He then goes on to point out that in designing knots there are two ways of achieving good proportion: either the design consists of a simple knot of a geometric pattern made up of interlacing threads; or the knot in the middle should be simple and there should be a border which consists of continuous interlacing threads. The moral here is an obvious one. Do not make your knot too complicated. Instead of looking as though it has been carefully thought out, it will seem a mess because the pattern will be too hard for the eye to unravel.

Markham says that the garden should be set out with close-growing evergreens, such as lavender, rosemary, germander, thyme and box and that the interlacing threads are made of different sorts of herbs which produce the necessary contrasts and emphasize the overs and unders.

He then mentions a lovely idea: the use of coloured earths to fill the spaces between the threads. Interestingly, the colours all have heraldic connotations, which points to the derivation of knot gardens from heraldic badges. To make yellow or 'armoury', he recommends that clay, sand or Flanders tiles should be beaten to dust; for white the coarsest chalk should be used; pure coal dust for black; broken bricks for red; white chalk and coal dust mixed together for blue, although I imagine the effect tends to be grey rather than blue. It is good advice to stick to these recipes for the pigments, even today. They are all 'earth' colours, which, as any painter knows, provide a very good background against which to build a composition. If you try brighter pigments you will end up with a background which leaps up at the onlooker and distracts attention from the subtle design of the plants. Incidentally, if you want to try coloured earths, remember that they really ought to be renewed each year if the knot is to be kept in perfect condition.

Sometimes the threads, though continuous, do not interlace. To quote Markham: 'I call broken quarters those many small parcels which are sundered and separate from one another...if you be disposed to plant any herbs in the midst of broken quarters, they must be short, as, pennyroyal, marjoram, camomile, daisies, violets, basil, rue, to give grace unto little squares.' A tall herb or little tree could go in the middle or at each corner, thus in my opinion reflecting the pendant bosses of Jacobean ceilings.

John Parkinson, writing in 1629, called broken quarters 'open knots' and said they should be planted with 'outlandish flowers', those recently introduced from abroad. The flowers can be picked to make nosegays. Parkinson sometimes used the word 'trayles' instead of threads and says that dead material can be used, such as lead, boards, bones, tiles or pebble stones.

For special forms in squares, they are as many, as there are devises in Gardeners' brains.
WILLIAM LAWSON 1617

Heere I have made the true Lovers Knott To ty it in Marriage was never my lott 'Cross Diamonds in the paper I doe frame And in the ground I can draw the same
STEPHEN BLAKE 1664

Another English writer who advocated knots as a garden feature was William Lawson. In 1618 he included a garden knot in his design for a small garden in the form of the Yorkist Rose combined with a six-pointed masonic star. He comments that the number of forms of knots and mazes is so great that the selection must be left to the discretion of the gardener. However we decide to reconstruct a sixteenth- or seventeenth-century knot garden, we must always bear in mind that it should be neat, symmetrical and not too complicated. 'You should keep your level to a hair, if you fail in this you fail in your whole work.' It should be a visual experience of pleasure and should achieve perfection for as much of the year as possible. If you use flowers to infill, try not to make them fussy, and above all use plants grown in Tudor and Stuart gardens.

Famous Knot Gardens

When garden making, it is always an inspiration to visit other gardens. At the Brooklyn Botanic Garden, New York, at Filoli near San Francisco, at Hampton Court and at New Place, Stratford, there are knots laid out from old patterns (but sometimes infilled with modern plants). The Brooklyn knot is a splendid affair with coloured gravel; at Stratford the overall effect is charming, with sunken beds, railings and a covered alley constructed from 'carpenter's work'. At Cranborne there is a knot delightfully filled with old-fashioned plants and has a period air—you feel that Tradescant could well have designed and planted it himself. It is small, intimate and close to the house, and it is easy to imagine the lady of the house approving of her new garden. At Hatfield House there is a knot on a larger scale, in a wonderful site with raised paths all round looking down on to it, beside the

Below: **The knot at the Brooklyn Botanical Garden, New York.**

Bottom left: **The knot at the National Herb Garden, Washington D.C.**

Bottom right: **The open knot in the garden of Moseley Old Hall, Staffordshire in a pattern very reminiscent of strapwork on a ceiling. Notice the covered alley of carpenter's work along one side.**

Bishop's Palace. Hatfield is steeped in history and the magical spirit of the place has been caught; the plant patterns all echo the Elizabethan age, but also show flair passed down for the present. The National Trust has reconstructed two knot gardens: one at Moseley Old Hall, the other at Little Moreton Hall. Both have been accurately carried out from seventeenth-century designs, using box as the thread and standards of box to represent the pendant bosses. Black polythene has been laid under the gravel to eliminate weeds, and the beds are edged with wooden boards. Both are highly successful.

At Tudor House in Southampton there is a most vibrant and successful reproduction of a Tudor garden. Step into it and you immediately feel yourself transported back four centuries. The central feature is a knot derived from the *Maison Rustique*, with four inter-lacing shields. In the house you will find the same pattern carved over the sixteenth-century fireplace, so naturally it was copied outside in teucrium, box and sweet-smelling herbs.

At the risk of repeating myself, do not be afraid of the old gardening books, particularly if you are interested in knot gardens. After looking at some of the best of today's re-created knots, you should be able to work out what some of the most ambiguous descriptions mean, for the writer often assumes that their readers understand the subject and so do not bother to explain fully. But they do repay some thought. One expression which has puzzled me indicates that if flowers of only one colour are used then they will look like 'divers coloured ribbons'. But then, reading Samuel Gilbert (1682), one realizes that the threads could well be double instead of single and have flowers planted between them, in which case the colour of the flowers would repeat the lines of the design rather than infill it. The result would then be a pattern of 'divers coloured ribbons', and very pretty too.

Above: **The knot at Tudor House, Southampton.**

Above: **The design on which the Tudor House knot is based taken from** *La Maison Rustique* **(1583).**

Left: **A knot of the same design at Barnsley House, shown in its early stages.**

CHAPTER SIX

BEDS AND BORDERS

Two of my grandchildren came to me very seriously one day last summer and said that they had watched me walking slowly round the garden and they wondered what I had been thinking. It was their next remark which took my breath away. 'We'll push you around in a wheel-chair when you get too old to walk—if you'll tell us about your flowers.'

Fair enough. I took them into the house and showed them the picture in Humphry Repton's book showing a raised bed filled with strawberries growing at a height at which the elderly man in his wheel-chair could see, pick and enjoy them.

This set me thinking. I hope that they may read this one day, for I am sure I did not tell them about the untold pleasures of having a garden which is pleasing from all the windows of the house, one which you can walk round at every season of the year and find something beautiful to appreciate, a garden full of surprises. They think of our garden as splendid for hide-and-seek, with plenty of hedges and hidden corners.

You may have a garden with only water, grass, trees, paths, an occasional statue and a patio, but this to me would not be a real garden. There must be flowers even if there are only a few. This chapter, then, is about, making beds and borders and filling them with flowers for your delight: 'The ordering of the garden of pleasure', as John Parkinson wrote three and a half centuries ago. We have so many more flowers available to us than he had, but much has happened since then and our concepts of a garden have grown more complicated.

'Fourscore yards square for the fruit, and thirty for the Flower-garden, will be sufficient for a nobleman; but for a private gentleman, forty for the one, and twenty for the other will be sufficient.'

JOHN REA, 1665.

Medieval Beds and Borders

Walafrid Strabo—'Walafrid the squint-eyed' was born in AD 809. He was abbot of Reichenau, a Benedictine monastery, and his two great talents were for writing Latin verse and for gardening. In his poem *Hortulus*, or *The Little Garden*, he describes his gardening activities.

I set to with my mattock
And dug up the sluggish ground. From their embraces
I tore those nettles though they grew and grew again.
I destroyed the tunnels of the moles that haunt dark places,
And back to the realms of light I summoned the worms.
Then my small patch was warmed by winds from the south
And the sun's heat. That it should not be washed away,
We faced it with planks and raised it in oblong beds
A little above the ground.

So we know that in the ninth century the monks were growing their plants in oblong, raised beds faced with planks. No other words tell us this so clearly. Through the Middle Ages there are many illustrations showing this, but these beds were made to grow flowers for picking rather than as attractive displays in themselves. Looking through a selection of illustrations we find that flowers were sparsely planted in these raised beds or were grown in turf on higher beds which could also be used as seats.

These higher turfed beds were arranged around the perimeter of the garden. Behind would be a wall or trellis up which flowers—often roses—grew. In some other illustrations these high beds are isolated in the middle of flowery meads, always with brickwork sides. Square beds were sometimes arranged in chess-board fashion, probably in order to grow one herb in each square.

In the sixteenth century, the main pattern of the knot garden was often surrounded by a border of continuous, interlacing herbs. It was literally the straight frame enclosing the knot. Not until the seventeenth century did beds with curved contours become fashionable. Typical examples of these are represented in the frontispiece of the Dutch book *Hortus Floridus* by Crispin de Passe (1614) and in the garden of the Castle of Idstein, near Frankfurt-am-Main; in both cases the beds were random in shape. At about the same time in England William Lawson recommends curved beds which are geometric in design.

The difference in meaning between the two words, bed and border is interesting. It is most clearly stated in the works of the two late seventeenth-century writers, John Worlidge and John Rea. Worlidge declares that borders are the edging to grass plots. Rea, in describing a walled square garden, recommends a series of straight sided beds, in the middle, but 'the borders about the walls' should be level with the beds. They should still be edged with planks, and the planting should still be rather sparse. Flowers, in fact, played a subservient part to the design of the beds, except in gardens where 'florist' flowers were grown.

In the next century flowers played no part in the schemes of the landscape designers, but in smaller gardens such as Newnham Courtney, town gardens, parsonage and manor house gardens and the 'flower garden' as mentioned by John Hill in his book *Eden* in 1757 there were beds and borders near the house and also beds carved out of the lawn. Hill dedicated his book to the Earl of Bute. He in turn was working in close conjunction with Princess Augusta at Kew, where there were beds and borders laid out to contain the many newly introduced plants from the east coast of North America.

Hill makes a distinction between the flower garden and the pleasure garden, the latter being the transition from the flower garden to the wilderness and meandering walks. Sir William Chambers, also closely connected with Kew, explains in his *Dissertation on Oriental Gardening* the importance of the arrangement of flowers: 'Avoid all sudden transitions both with regard to dimension and colour; rising gently from the smallest flowers to hollyhocks, paeonies, sunflowers, carnation poppies and others of the boldest growth, and vary the tints by easy gradation from white, straw-colour, purple and incarnate, to the deepest blues and most brilliant crimsons and scarlets.'

Above: The Spring Garden from the *Hortus Floridus* (1614) by Crispin de Passe showing a typical open knot with sparse planting in the beds, and surrounded by an enclosed alley with arbours at the corners.

Left: The Queen's Garden parterre at Kew, executed in 1964, from a seventeenth-century design by Jacques Androuet du Cerceau.

Many plants were reaching England in the latter half of the eighteenth century, and their introduction played an important part in the new development of our gardens. There were two distinct trends: the new flowers were either grown for their beauty or, as at the Chelsea Physic Garden where Philip Miller was curator, for their botanical interest. A study of some of the nurserymen's catalogues of the time gives one an insight into the ever-increasing number of plants available to late eighteenth-century gardeners.

'The bedded-out plants are plants with no association as regards the past. No poet ever sang their beauty, and no legend tells the origin of their birth.'

HENRY BRIGHT, 1881.

Nineteenth-Century Borders

Writing in the 1830s John Loudon says, 'The modern style is a collection of irregular groups and masses, placed about the house as a medium, uniting it with the open lawn.' Trees in eighteenth-century landscapes were planted in clumps in the picturesque manner. With the general change in fashion, flowers and shrubs too were planted in the lawns in groups near the house, the beds cut of turf or surrounded with gravel. For this new style Loudon invented the word 'gardenesque'.

Loudon is full of advice. The grass paths between the beds should be broad in order to prevent a fussy, overcrowded look; there should be gravel walks to use on wet days. The shape of the beds should include no acute angles, except where the whole design might be seen from above. 'The best form is the circle, provided that it be always kept of small size, say from 18 in – 6 ft [50 – 180 cm] in diameter, and one circle never to be placed nearer to another than 2 ft [60 cm] and that these beds be thrown together in groups and constellations, as stars are in a firmament, or single trees and single shrubs in a well-planted park.'

BEDDING OUT

From 1845, when the tax was removed from glass, and heating systems had been improved for glass houses, the fashion for bedding out took over. The surest way of discovering what plants were used is from contemporary monthly magazines. A nobleman's flower gardener near London in 1850 used pelargoniums (nothing he says exceed these fine flowers for bedding), bovardias, cupheas, anagallis, lobelias, alonsoas, penstemons, several roses, calceolarias, dianthus, fuchsias, hydrangeas, petunias and *Phlox drummondii*. In 1860, Shirley Hibberd's magazine *The Floral World* had no less than ten major entries on bedding plants including 'bedding for next year' and 'Preservation of bedding plants in a cold pit'. In June that year 'geraniums and verbenas are being almost given away.' Supply finally exceeded demand. Finally carpet bedding became the rage, using succulents and dwarf coloured-leaf plants such as iresines and altenantheras.

Carpet bedding at Broughton Castle, Oxfordshire in about 1910. Note the topiary peacock.

John Fleming, gardener to Harriet, Duchess of Sutherland at Cliveden, went one better than his fellow head gardeners and had a 'system' of floral decoration which he called 'Spring and Winter Flower Gardening'. For spring he used anemones, alyssium, iberis, polyanthus, pansies and tulips. White crocus and white daisies were grown near the ribbon of ivy. In another bed he has myosotis, yellow jonquil, mixed anemones, *Narcissus poeticus* and yellow tulips. Another combination was a broad belt of *Aubrieta purpurea*, and behind this a mixture of snowdrops, crocus, winter aconite, hepatica, pansies, mixed tulips and jonquils. Behind these was a broad row of single Italian wallflowers. Quite an array it must have made. It must have also created a lot of work.

Mr. Fleming put much thought into his winter garden arrangements, for, as he comments great energies were devoted to making the flower garden bright for the summer months. 'It is however soon over; and then comes a much longer space, with nothing to look upon but the bare soil of the beds, in bad contrast, oftentimes, with the beautiful green sward with which they are surrounded. In the dull months we must use berries and foliage, and with the first approach of spring a few sprigs of heath.' He suggests using *Pernettya mucronata, Skimmia japonica* and mahonia, the golden- leaf honeysuckle, ivies, aucuba, yew both golden and green. The blooming plants should be *Jasminum nudiflorum* and a selection of heaths. These are only a few of his suggestions but they amply demonstrate that, in the 1860s, attempts were being made to create interest in the garden all through the year.

Shirley Hibberd was one of the first influential characters to write against carpet bedding and the excessive use of tender plants. His magazine *The Floral World* first appeared in 1858, and cost 4*d.* By 1864 he was pointing out that too much of the gardener's time was occupied in raising bedding plants at the expense of general horticulture. If bedding is prohibited by the owner then 'noble clumps of fragrant white lilies, patches of Christmas rose, double daisy, polyanthus, primulas, Solomon's Seal...and thousands of other interesting subjects' would be restored to the neglected borders.

In 1871 William Robinson started his monthly magazine, *The Garden*, and he too took up the battle against bedding out. This debate remains unresolved, but with true English compromise we have mixed borders today. We use shrubs and perennials and leave spaces for bulbs, wallflowers and forget-me-nots. Later we can fill those same spaces with antirrhinums, petunias and tobacco plants. There is little new in gardening, we merely adapt old ideas in the distinctive manner of our age.

Border Design Today

Beds and borders, their siting and shape, are essential features in our garden design. This must always be a personal aspect of gardening and these are just a few of my thoughts which arise from everyday observations and my reactions while walking round my garden. Is the satisfaction to be had from practical gardening more important than the aesthetic

An Edwardian border in July full of herbaceous and annual plants in cottage-garden style. Note that each pathway is flanked by terracotta pots full of nasturtiums and how the garden is entered through rose-covered archways.

pleasure of the result? To my mind it is the latter, however, the former must not be for-gotten. I like to have beds which are a pleasure to look at from my bedroom window and my desk, all through the year. To achieve this they must have an architectural design both in shape and planting—but they should have far more than this; from spring to autumn there must be colour, and in winter they should have form.

APPROACHING THE HOUSE

An important planting is the one which you see each time that you arrive home, either as you drive to the garage, or, if you have a cottage garden, as you walk up the path towards your front door. If you are driving the planting you see should be bold and striking—a combination of shapes interspersed with blocks of seasonal colour or differing textured leaves. Something bold, simple but pleasing. We have upright evergreens, *Chamaecyparis* 'Elwoodii' alternating with grey mounds of santolina, the latter clipped back hard in March. The whole bed is a mass of daffodils, *Narcissus* 'Golden Harvest', planted decades ago, which dominate the scene for three weeks in April while the santolina puts on the new growth. It is not the sort of bed along which one walks in contemplation. It looks well from a distance and complements the façade of the house. It is simple, has a defined and regular form and takes very little upkeep each year.

If, on the other hand, you arrive at your front gate and walk to the house along a narrow, straight path then you will want to fill beds either side with overflowing cottage-garden flowers, sweet-smelling permanent plants, old favourites like lavender and pinks, daphnes and roses. Each time you walk up your path you will observe new growth and will become familiar with the smallest detail—spring flowers pushing through the ground, primroses and dwarf daffodils and iris. As these fade they leave space for summer flowers —sweet williams, antirrhinums, petunias, nasturtiums; any that may take your fancy. The annuals will have a longer flowering time than perennials such as campanulas and sedums, but then they require more work; you must choose for yourself. Twin beds each side of the path, small though they may be, can give endless pleasure and have a distinctive character. I think that I would choose a simple but formal approach; neatly trimmed, box edging patterned with box balls and pyramids, clipped bays and standard roses, no hybrid teas but elegant small-flowered varieties like *Rosa* 'Little White Pet' and *Rosa* 'Ballerina'.

Standards of *Rosa* 'Little White Pet' as a central feature in the vegetable garden at Barnsley House.

For scent I would have groups of lilies, selecting whichever best suited the soil. At their feet would be violets, pansies and scented heliotropes. I like to be able to brush through my plants, sometimes touching them to trap their perfume. In the narrow beds under my windows and beside the front door there would be honeysuckles, rosemary, more roses, clematis and bay trees. The satisfactory thing is that it is all small enough for me to keep in spotless condition, without a sign of a weed. I could have two more borders each side of my front garden, where I would have the taller flowers, hollyhocks, fennel, angelica, old-fashioned sweet peas, phlox and monarda. A few evergreen shrubs would give winter interest—osmanthus and sarcococca, holly and hebes. There will, of course, be a corner which gets less sunshine; here there will be patches of lily of the valley and hellebores. It will be quite ordinary and simple to manage, just as a cottage garden should be, but it will have plenty of thought and fertilizer bestowed upon it.

A Driveway Bed

There is another type of entrance to a property which necessitates thoughtful planting. If there is space enough for cars to drive in and park you should try to work out a scheme which includes an interesting bed on one side of the parking area. I dislike central beds surrounded by gravel; they remind me of seaside hotels or grand houses where the guests are dropped off and the car continues its journey round a circular Victorian rock bed. One corner is sure to face south or get a good quota of sunlight. Mark out this patch and make certain that you allow enough turning room for the car. When you are satisfied, build a low wall, just high enough to stop cars driving on to your plants and to give you an opportunity to plant some tumbling plants. Avoid bedding-out plants, except as infillers, and stick to foliage plants and those which look good for a considerable part of the year.

Start by making a list. It should include evergreen shapes, bold leaves, reliable perennials, especially those with evergreen leaves such as *Tiarella cordifolia* and bergenias, shrubs which have berries or fruit such as *Callicarpa giraldii* with its unusual violet berries. This is an opportunity to grow heathers too, which can make a wonderful splash in February and March. Three more reliable hardies which would make for interest are the Westonbirt dogwood, *Cornus alba* 'Sibirica', with rich red stems in winter, a variegated holly, *Ilex x altaclarensis* 'Lawsoniana', and a mahonia for scent. If there is enough space, one slow-growing upright evergreen such as *Juniperus communis Hibernica* and one deciduous tree with not too dense foliage, *Gleditschia triacanthos* 'Sunburst' would add dimension.

Do not plant a weeping willow unless you intend moving after five years. It cannot be pruned back, whereas the gleditschia can have a yearly clip to keep it shapely. Decide on your colour scheme and draw out a rough plan. Mark this out on the ground, starting with bamboo canes to represent your shrubs, then take a critical look, first from the entrance gate, then from the front door (you must give your visitors a good view while they wait for you to answer the door), and then maybe from your sitting-room window—all the places, in fact, from which it will regularly be seen.

In many of my favourite homes the main axis of the house runs from the front door straight on, through the hall and maybe the living room, to another door which leads out into the garden proper. To walk from the comparative shadow of the house and then out into sunlight can have a wonderful impact.

As you step into your garden you become full of expectation; this is the point from which the garden should radiate and be planned. You cannot alter the plan of your house but you can make a starting point for your garden from the door through which you enter it. There should be a vista from here, perhaps through a series of garden 'rooms', each room with its own beds and borders backed by hedges, trees or the garden fence. Whatever the plan, your eye should be led on, inducing you to step out to discover the further pleasures which await you.

'In every garden four things are necessary to be provided for, flowers, fruit, shade and water, and whoever lays out a garden without all these must not pretend to any perfection. It ought to lie to the best parts of the house, so as to be but like one of the rooms out of which you step into another. The part of your garden next to your house should be a parterre for flowers, and grass-plots bordered with flowers...'

Sir William Temple, 1685.

Top: The thornless rose 'Zepherine Drouhin', one of the most beautiful for mid-June flowering.

Bottom: One of the most reliable and sweetly scented honeysuckles, *Lonicera Periclymenum* 'Belgica'.

Opposite: A June view caught in early morning light from the drawing-room door at Barnsley House looking along the path of rock roses flanked by Irish yews. It is an attractive idea to continue the main axis of the house through one of the doorways into the garden.

BY THE HOUSE

Try to have interesting plants in the border under the house—those which your horticultural friends will wish to pause beside and discuss. It will probably be quite narrow so that you can tend the wall shrubs which you have growing up the house. More than likely, it will face in a southerly direction. I believe that this is one of the most important borders in the garden but it is also the most difficult. A climbing rose is essential—'Zepherine Drouhin' is a wise choice by the door as it is thornless and will not hurt you, and it flowers early in the summer. Honeysuckle is a must; *Lonicera periclynenum* 'Belgica', the early Dutch variety, will reach your bedroom window and fill your room with evening scent. For clematis I would choose a spring-flowering macropetala or *C. alpina* 'Frances Rivis' with its deep blue, nodding flowers. If you have a sheltered spot then try *C. cirrhosa var. balearica*,, the fern-leafed clematis, to flower in March. My two favourites for late flowering are *C. viticella* 'Minuet' and *C.v.* 'Royal Velour', both of these require hard pruning in spring so you will not have untidy straggling growth. The Passion Flower, *Passiflora caerulea*, has an interesting and beautiful flower and is fragrant. It is almost evergreen and climbs by tendrils so needs a host plant, wires or trellis to support it. Wisteria will eventually dominate the scene unless it is strictly pruned (if it does not flower it is likely that the house sparrows are pecking away the buds). My advice is to keep off rampant growers, they may swamp your treasures. You want plenty of detail here.

Having decided on your climbers you can concentrate on a few low shrubs and specialities. I would choose *Azara microphylla*, knowing full well that it will get too big, but it needs a warm spot and its scent is marvellous. This is also the place for *Myrtus communis*, the common myrtle. It is one of my essential shrubs, but as it will not stand too much frost you must keep cuttings in reserve. Some of the smaller cistus would go well, as would grey shrubs such as *Ballota pseudodictanmus*, *Convolvulus cneorum*, *Hebe albicans*, and *Perovskia x* 'Blue Spire'. You should infill with individual plants which you can enjoy and are less common; auriculas and gold-laced polyanthus, perhaps *Teucrium crispum* and *Morina longifolia*, the latter an imposing plant with a rosette of prickly evergreen leaves and spikes of 2½ ft (76 cm) pale pink flowers. I try to keep a space for scented-leafed geraniums to be dropped in during summer. The whole point, in my opinion, is to make this border a home for your most interesting plants, ones that would get lost in the medley of a larger bed away from the house.

THE DIFFERENCE BETWEEN BEDS AND BORDERS

As we move on from near the house into the main part of your garden we should again pause and consider the differences between beds and borders. A border, as its name suggests, is an adjunct or component of something else. It is the decorative surround to another feature, in this case probably the lawn. It need not be on more than one side of the lawn and will have a backing in the form of a fence, yew hedge or wall. This wall or hedge is like a backdrop of stage scenery which helps to set off the 'players in the piece'. I think of a bed as a free-standing area which can be of any shape or size. The 'cast' on the stage have no benefits of any immediate scenery. They must rely on their own offerings to create a beautiful composition.

Two examples spring to mind, first the 'Red borders' at Hidcote in Gloucestershire, which run each side of a wide grass path and are backed, one by a wall and the other by a hedge. The backing invites a planting of tall shrubs, designed for its general effect. You would never call these the 'Red beds'. The other example are the 'Island beds' made famous at the Bressingham Gardens at Diss in Norfolk which the talented Bloom family have created with the express purpose of displaying their plants to best advantage. I do not mean by this that plants in borders need not play an individual role. They must, but they are usually planted in a colour scheme or groups for their total effect. Think of Gertrude Jekyll and William Robinson colour schemes, the long twin herbaceous borders at Arley Hall

in Cheshire and borders in many of the great National Trust gardens. From midsummer through until autumn they make an impact upon you from wherever you see them—or that is their intended purpose. You walk round a bed but walk along a border. The planting principles are much the same in both except for the element of height. In a border this will be consistent. It will in general pile up from front to back, allowing for poetic licence to create some minor undulations and small vistas. The old-fashioned herbaceous borders were labour intensive in the summer months, with necessary staking, but this can be minimized both by choice of plants and by the use of shrubs and even small trees. Hibiscus could take the place of tall michaelmas daisies, the upright-growing *Prunus serrulata erecta* 'Amanogawa' would give spring colour and then act as a support for an autumn flowering *Clematis texensis* or *Cl. viticella*. Sweet peas can use the skeletons of *Crambe cordifolia* as climbing posts. These are but ideas, others you may work out for yourself.

No one can deny that a well filled flower garden, with a bright season, is very beautiful. It is, however, soon over. Then comes a much longer space, with nothing to look upon but the bare soil of the beds, in bad contrast, oftentimes, with the beautiful green sward with which they are surrounded.

JOHN FLEMING 1870

ISLAND BEDS

Bedding plants presumably got their name because they are used for bedding out. They are 'in-and-out plants' and their natural place is in flower beds especially made for them, to provide a bright display of colour for as long a period in the year as possible. Such beds are common in parks and public gardens but are out of fashion in private gardens. Flower beds suggest to me a planting of not too tall herbaceous subjects, combined with low shrubs and, in special circumstances, an upright evergreen, a medium-sized deciduous tree or a clump of bamboos or pampas grass to create an accent from which the planting radiates. The element of added height is not essential and can in fact be overstressed. It depends upon the surroundings as beds are often sited so you can look over and beyond them to another feature. They are part of the total design.

As far as planting is concerned it can follow all the same thoughts that you have when designing your borders, but restricting your choice to lower plants. The actual height will relate to the width of the bed. When you are planning a border you have to think of the effect from one side only and from each end, but with your island bed you will see it from every angle, all round.

The backbone of your island bed will be hardy perennials. Choose these according to your soil. There is no future in putting plants which like a well-drained situation into heavy clay or acid lovers into a lime soil. Make notes of flowers and foliage you admire in catalogues and when you visit gardens. Good books on plants make excellent winter reading. Your 'see-through' plants (a Christopher Lloyd expression) will be important. I mean those which flower on bare stems above a rosette of leaves. My best examples of these are *Verbena bonariensis* and the herbaceous *Phlomis russeliana*, (*P. samia* and *P. viscosa*). The seed heads make perfect perching posts for the birds in winter.

'Flower beds are often best set in grass, and those who care to see them will approach them quite as readily on grass as on hard walks.'

WILLIAM ROBINSON, 1883.

COLOUR

If you are a beginner start with the tried old favourites, campanulas, delphiniums, monarda (bergamot), penstemon, iris, hardy geraniums, fuchsias and geums. Look out for plants with a long flowering period which will fit into your own colour scheme. In gardening, as in any skill, you cannot run before you can walk. You learn slowly, by study and by experiment, about both flowers and leaves. Gertrude Jekyll knew as much about colour in the garden as any other writer, because she trained as an artist before she made her famous garden at Munstead Wood and before she wrote her books. The following paragraph contains the essence of her colour philosophy as she used it with plants. 'At the two ends [of the border] there is a groundwork of grey and glaucous foliage... with this... there are flowers of pure blue, grey-blue, white, palest yellow and palest pink; each colour partly in distinct masses and partly inter-grouped. The colouring then passes through stronger yellows to orange and red... The the colour recedes in an inverse sequence through orange and deep yellow to pale yellow, white and palest pink; again with blue-grey foliage. At

Island beds at Bloom's Nurseries, Norfolk.

this end, instead of the pure blues we have purples and lilacs. Then passing along the path next the border the value of the colour arrangement is still more strongly felt. Each portion now becomes a picture in itself, and every one is of such colouring that it best prepares the eye, in accordance with natural law, for what is to follow. Standing for a few moments before the endmost region of grey and blue, and saturating the eye to its utmost capacity with these colours, it passes with extraordinary avidity to the succeeding yellows. These intermingle in a pleasant harmony with reds and scarlets, blood reds and clarets and then lead to the yellows. Now the eye has become saturated, this time with rich colouring, and has therefore, by law of complementary colour, acquired a strong appetite for the greys and purples. These therefore assume an appearance of brilliancy that they would not have had without the preparation provided by their recently received complementary colour.'

This may sound rather too complex for smaller beds, but I would apply it to both beds and borders in the following way. Start your planting with a mound of grey *Santolina incana* or a yucca as Miss Jekyll suggests, to make a good feature for the corner, surround this with blue and white flowers, *Erigeron* 'Prosperity' (a light blue), *Iberis* 'Snowflake' and a white and a blue dwarf phlox. There are several free flowering campanulas in shades of blue and white which would look well in front. Love-in-the-mist (*Nigella*) seed scattered will fill in odd gaps. *Platycodon grandiflorum,* the balloon flower, comes in white and blue, while for more height you could plant *Echinops ritro*, the blue globe thistle. Acanthus is always a wonderful value plant with its splendid leaves and long lasting flower spikes. Warm yellows and yellowy greens should come next, but still keeping a thread of grey with *Anaphalis yedoensis, Artemisia* 'Silver Queen', and *A.* 'Lambrook Silver', both about 30

62 BEDS AND BORDERS

The carefully planned 'Red'
borders at Hidcote,
Gloucestershire.

The long twin borders at Arley
Hall, Cheshire are among the
earliest in England and date back
to 1846.

Top left: Grey foliage used to good effect.
Stachys lanata surrounds an old and shapely bush of *Santolina incana*. The dark green leaves of a self-sown *Helleborus foetidus* make a pleasing contrast with the mass of grey.

Top right: The filigree grey foliage of *Achillea* 'Moonshine' is attractive even when the plant is not in flower.

Bottom left: *Yucca gloriosa*, a useful feature plant, often used by Gertrude Jekyll as a point of emphasis at the end of her borders.

Bottom right: The pink mallow (*Lavatera olbia* 'Rosea') a useful fast-growing shrub in bloom throughout the summer. However, its bright colour is not to everyone's taste and can prove difficult to blend with other strong colours.

in (75 cm) high, and *A. pontica* for a carpet in front. *Achillea* 'Moonshine' is a strong yellow and the foliage almost grey. There is a good selection of yellow coreopsis all of which are long flowering and make tidy clumps. They are good for cutting too. A collection of day lilies (*Hemerocallis*) would come now in their wide choice of yellows and orange and amber to lead on to the orange-reds and scarlets, using *Lychnis calcedonica* and *Potentilla* 'Gibson's Scarlet' and thence to the blue reds or crimsons and pinks of phlox and monardas. Then we return to the greys and purples. Gertrude Jekyll never mixed blue with purple, for in the spectrum blue-greens merge towards yellows and blue-purples towards crimson. (Some reds have blue in their make-up and others have yellow: these two do not mix well.) *Salvia superba* 'East Friesland' must not go beside *S. patens*, the latter a true blue. Many of the annuals have striking colours and they mix in well with your perennials if you have time to raise them from seed, or scatter this about in between. The convenient thing about perennials is how easy they are to move in the autumn.

LOW SHRUBS

Low shrubs suitable for your island beds and borders are those which have a naturally good shape or can be kept trim by clipping. Both the grey and the purple sage are indispensables, so are rue, *Ruta graveolens*, most of the spiraeas, especially the two relatively new varieties *S. bulmalda* 'Goldflame' and *S. japonica* 'Little Princess'. The former, is a startling sight, as its leaves develop in spring—rich gold combined with streaks of crimson. One plant of this is no good, you need a group of three to make a firm enough impact and not just be startling. 'Little Princess' is a useful infiller for later in the year and makes a mound of rose-crimson flowers.

I like to use *Lonicera nitida* 'Baggerson's Gold' and the golden form of privet. Both add substance to the border and can be kept to any size or shape you wish. You can grow clematis through the privet, either spring or autumn flowering. Fuchsias can be used with discretion and must have bulbs or early flowering plants such as forget-me-nots to cover the ground before the fuchsias emerge, I have mentioned *Santolina incana*; the variety *S. neapolitana* has more elegant leaves but a rather less tidy overall appearance.

For spikes, yuccas and phormiums (New Zealand flax) are useful. Miss Jekyll used yuccas to great effect; they are plants which improve with age both in size and flowering, but I am a bit dubious as to the hardiness of phormiums. I believe they come into the catagory of plants which need protection during their early years and thereafter become tougher, when they have 'got their roots down'. Phormiums are plants I would persevere with as when they are good they are very, very good and add style to your bed, especially when they flower. I do not like berberis in the bed, it is much too prickly and unfriendly when weeding. Both varieties of ceratostigma are useful for August and September provided they have enough sun and are given earlier-flowering companions. Generally I am not enthusiastic about broom in the border for when it is over it is dull and even unattractive. There are the right places for it such as banks and the wild garden. I would not like to be without the Spanish broom, *Spartium junceum*, for its marvellous drifting honey scent which can pervade a corner of the garden and surprise you if there is a hedge between you and it. Prune back its rush-like stems in the autumn or it will become extremely leggy. It is easy to grow from seed so you can keep a supply handy.

The pink mallow, *Lavatera olbia* 'Rosea', makes as long a show as any shrub in the border, with loose sprays of hollyhock-like flowers from June until October. I have found one in a cottage garden with a much prettier coloured flower, a less harsh pink flushed with white. Another pink shrub for the border, but probably too tall for the bed, is the American Beauty Bush, *Kolkwitzia amabilis*. This flowers in June so can have a later blooming rose such as *R.* 'New Dawn' or an autumn *Clematis texensis* or *C. tangutica* growing through it. A reliable shrub for the middle of the border is *Olearia x scilloniensis*, the daisy bush. It is completely clothed in small white aster-like flowers in May and June and the grey leaves are an added attraction. The lacecap and hortensis hydrangeas are not for the mixed bed or border but the late-flowering *Hydrangea villosa* is a lovely porcelain blue with lavender florets and associates well with pink *Anemone japonica* and with acanthus.

Hebes are a great standby. For the front *Hebe albicans* with grey leaves and white flowers is reliable. *H. rakaiensis (sub-alpina)* grows into so perfect a low dome that it appears to have been shaped. I like it on a corner or at the end of a border. *H.* 'Great Orme' needs to be tucked in to afford it some winter shelter. It is useful for its bright eye-catching pink flowers. *H. salicifolia*, one of the hardiest, is free-flowering and the most sweetly scented of the hebes, but is too tall for an island bed.

I have never grown ling or heathers, probably because all are lime haters except the winter flowerers and *Erica terminalis*. This does not mean that I do not admire a heather garden, especially whole beds of them together, but I do not admire them planted in a small group at the front of and around herbaceous plants.

RAISED BORDERS

I have written about raised beds in Chapter Ten on 'The Rock Garden'. In certain circumstances raised borders suit herbaceous plants and shrubs which demand good drainage. They also help when a garden is flat and needs additional height. Two special gardens come to my mind. In one, as you pass through an opening in a Cotswold stone wall, there is a short avenue of flowering cherries in front of you and on each side of these are sunken lawns. As you look right and left you see dramatic herbaceous borders along the wall—dramatic because they are raised about 18 in (45 cm) with stone retaining walls, and the already tall Pacific hybrid delphiniums look like giants. They have nepeta (catmint) at their feet which hangs over the retaining wall and great mounds of *Senecio* 'Sunshine'. If the border were at ground level it would lose much of its quality, and equally if tall plants had not been chosen the effect of height would have been minimized.

The other is a small garden, and the purpose of making a raised bed at one side was two-fold. It gave an opportunity to incorporate a well-drained soil to grow grey plants, cistus and other sun-loving flowers, and it immediately added an element of style to the garden. Halfway along the border are two steps leading up to a seat, and the border is divided lengthways by a narrow brick and stone path. The wall at the back is completely covered with honeysuckles, roses and clematis, so when you are sitting on the seat you feel enclosed by flowers and scents. The front sections are filled with plants which enjoy attention and are best seen at close quarters, and many of them hang down.

The raised bed described in the text made by Alvilde Lees-Milne at Essex House, Badminton, Avon. Here it is photographed in its first summer before the edging plants have had time to spill over the low wall. Notice the use of the trellis-work above the wall to add extra height for climbers.

The raised beds at Sudeley Castle, Gloucestershire can accomodate larger shrubs because of greater size, but should not completely hide the beautiful old wall behind.

Pampas grass requires careful placing. Here in the late Sir Frederick Gibberd's garden it adds style, emphasis and height at the end of a border.

GRASSES

Grasses make good bed and border plants, all belonging to the *Gramineae* family. They are fascinating plants with a diversity of colour, texture and leaf shape not contained in any other one family. To most people grass is just a green sward but a wander around the grass border at Kew can be an eye-opener and compel you to re-appraise the uses to which this family may be put. They range from tall pampas, usually grown as a spot plant in a round island bed in the middle of a suburban garden lawn, to the little emerald green spiky clumps of *Festula scorparia* which looks like a hedgehog emerging from a pot of green paint. Their movement is so graceful and they are surprisingly resilient to heavy winds which would snap other more rigid stems.

Among those we grow without a problem is *Milium effusum* 'Aureum', Bowles' Golden Grass, a non-invasive grass which will increase rather than decrease and, looks wonderful in spring with its fresh golden new foliage. It needs sunlight to be at its best, and will colonize under clumps of tree peonies. Years ago I bought seed of the annual *Briza maxima*. This was started in a border but has since moved itself into paving where it disperses its seeds each autumn after I have gathered enough of its nodding seed heads for drying. All the *Festuca* varieties are excellent for the front of a border and make upright accents among creeping thymes or creeping jenny, *Lysimachia nummularia* 'Aurea'.

To learn about grasses you should visit a botanical garden, Great Dixter in Sussex, Beth Chatto's remarkable garden in Essex, or Bloom's nurseries. I believe that a whole bed of grasses in a private garden would be rather eccentric but, used with discretion in a bed or border, they can provide ground cover and distinction.

A SUNK GARDEN

If the purpose of a raised bed is to bring the flowers nearer to eye level or to make tall plants even taller, the purpose of a sunk garden is to give a perspective on the beds which is otherwise unobtainable. This suggests formal beds, such as those in the sunk garden at Hampton Court, where the beds are filled with seasonal bedding plants and spring bulbs. This is perhaps a natural evolvement from the raised walks which looked down upon the sixteenth-century knot garden. A perfect example of this can be seen at the Shakespeare Museum garden at Stratford-on-Avon. Sir Edwin Lutyens designed sunken gardens with attractive paving and beautifully contrived steps, leading down into Jekyll plantings.

Zantedeschia aethiopica var. 'Crowborough' makes a perfect feature plant, the shining green leaves setting off the white spathes.

An idea which has been in my mind for many years is the exciting thought of creating a place for plants on a vertical as well as a horizontal plane. These thoughts have come piecemeal as I have visited gardens and read articles. It started when I went to a garden in Oxfordshire where the owners were dedicated plant lovers but had only a tiny garden. They had dug out a rectangular path around an area of 20 x 14 ft (6 x 4.25 m) and perhaps 4 ft (1.25 m) wide. They threw the earth outwards and levelled this off. They were left with a central raised bed at the original level of the garden, a sunken pathway, and a surrounding area considerably higher than they started with. They built retaining walls for the central raised bed and the outer segment, leaving plenty of crevices for plants. What planting area they had lost became the path, but they had gained the vertical walls they had created. Study some of the Gertrude Jekyll and Lutyens photographs and designs for gardens in *Gardens for Small Country Houses* and you will notice that frequently they too did the same thing.

Loddon Lily (*Leucojum aestivum*) a spring-flowering beauty which will multiply if left undisturbed.

I was delighted when Roberto Berle Marx, the great Brazilian garden designer, made this point when lecturing on garden design in London recently. He emphasized that when you build a retaining wall it should be thought of as an area for planting, whatever its purpose.

I recalled later the garden owned and planned by the garden designer William H. Frederick at Wilmington, Delaware. The garden is on an incline and here is just what Marx was talking about. It makes use of every surface, covering each with plants. Whatever the size of your garden it may be made more interesting by imagining every possible place and space, vertical or horizontal, in which plants can play a part.

We should consider plants for every site, damp beds, dry beds, those in the sun and those in shade. My philosophy does not change. Make the easier plants the backbone of your design and build up your repertoire as you succeed. Damp borders are those around natural ponds and swampy areas and purpose-made ponds where damp beds have been created.

DAMP SOIL AND SHALLOW WATER

Of the few plants which will grow with their roots in permanently damp soil or shallow water, my favourite is *Zantedeschia aethiopica*, the arum lily. These are associated with coolhouse growing but are hardy in the south of England and, once established, will flourish in colder districts. Planted in deep mud in a pool they become a summer feature but will also do well at the water's edge so long as they are not allowed to dry out in summer. I know of a large clump, in a border beside a house, which never fails to send up flower spikes each July and August. The leaves disappear in winter and the crowns then given a mulching or protection. But far the most dramatic groups I have seen have been growing in water sufficiently deep to prevent the roots being frozen, such as those in the lake at Pusey House near Faringdon.

Another favourite is the buttercup-yellow marsh marigold, *Caltha palustris*. These are wonderful in spring, and later the round leaves and seed heads are pretty. They associate well with primulas and mimulus, the monkey musks. I am fond of the common *Mimulus guttatus* with its dappled brown-yellow flowers, but there are more exotic varieties such as *M.* 'Whitecroft Scarlet'. The water avens, *Geum rivale* 'Leonard's variety', has pink single flowers and enjoys a damp cool place. *Iris sibirica* make a wonderful show in a damp sunny bed in June; later the brown seed heads are handsome.

There are so many plants which do well in a moist, but not wet, sunny place that again I can mention only a few. The white *Aconitum x bicolor* 'Ivorine' which I had from Beth Chatto many years ago, is a noteworthy plant. *Campanula* 'Burghaltii' has a stylish tubular flower of lilac-grey. It is not easy to find but well worth searching for. Among the more easily obtainable flowers I would mention astilbes and astrantias, heucheras and hostas, all of which do best in a damp situation, as does *Euphorbia griffithii* 'Fire Glow'.

For a startling spring effect I love *Filipendula ulmaria* 'Aurea' for its glowing foliage. Another spring-flowering beauty is *Leucojum aestivum*. Bulbs of these were given to us dug up from a garden on the Loddon river and the label said 'Loddon Lily'.

Polemonium caeruleum is one of our June standbys, as any visitors to our garden must know. The seed was collected by my son in Palestine years ago when he was with Oleg Polunin, author of the definitive book on Mediterranean plants. Our strain has been distributed widely and is now seeding itself around many gardens.

There are two Lysimachias which are reliable and effective, in sunshine with a moist root run, *L. ephemerun* with its leathery leaves and mauve flower spikes. It is always in demand in our nursery when in flower. *L. cletheroides* has unusual arching spikes in an attractive off-white in late summer. Bergamot, *Monarda didyma*, is definitely one of my favourite plants. It revels in a rich, damp soil. Its colouring leans towards the blue-reds and pinks.

A plant which needs to remain undisturbed in order to build up a good clump is *Gentiana asclepiadea*, especially effective in September when other border plants are fading. It is a lovely gentian blue and is best grown from seed which must be allowed to become frosted for successful germination.

By 'damp shade' I mean those places where the soil does not dry out in summer and there is a covering of deciduous trees to allow winter sunshine to filter through, or the least sunny side of a hedge or wall. There is no shortage of plants which will succeed, notably aquilegias, foxgloves, Solomon's Seal, dicentras, beucheras, hostas and mertensia. Low-growing plants for the same situation are ajuga, polyanthus and primroses, the golden form of pennywort (*Lysimachia nummularia aurea*), and the lovely little woodland pea *Lathyrus vernus*.

DRY SOIL AND SHADE

Whatever the type of soil, if you have a really dry bed in full sun you will have to add organic material to improve its moisture retentiveness before planting. Horse or cow manure are best for the purpose. These days when so many people are keen on riding there cannot be many places in Britain too far from stables. Mushroom compost and spent hops will also serve.

Failing any of these, a load of topsoil will help, but make sure that you look at it before you buy. I have in mind a garden with new owners where there is no compost heap on which to rely. My advice in these circumstances is 'Start a compost heap at once, using every available form of waste which will eventually rot—kitchen waste, everything from the garden (save pernicious weeds and woody material), lawn mowings and even waste paper, as long as it is shredded and put in moist. If you can, buy a bale of straw and add a layer of this every so often. When you are starting it is the bulk that you want if the heap is to grow quickly. An important part of our autumn routine is the sweeping up of every fallen leaf. These are then stacked in a wire netting cage and by the following autumn we have a rich supply of leaf mould. We use this as a mulch over the flower beds and it not only makes the beds look good but helps to keep down the weeds as well as providing humus. One word of advice: if the leaves are quite dry when you stack them they will not rot.

'I should be careful not to crowd too many different plants into my stream-picture. Where the Forget-me-nots are it would be quite enough to see them and the double Meadow-Sweet, and some good hardy moisture-loving Fern, Osmunda or Lady Fern.' GERTRUDE JEKYLL.

To return to the dry bed. Having given it an injection of some sort of stimulant, think of the plants which grow naturally in these circumstances, in Mediterranean countries, in coastal areas of California and high on stony hillsides in England. There are the grey plants and cistuses, iris and asphodels, nerines and oenothera, poppies, potentilla and yuccas, thymes and ferula. Some euphorbia require damp soil but *E. myrsinites* likes to have a dry root run and is excellent for flopping over the front of your border, while *E. characias* is a fine statuesque plant for a dominating situation. Dianthus and rock roses (helianthemums) like sun and dryness and so do the sedums and zauschneria, the Californian trumpet plant.

Dry shade is usually caused by trees taking moisture from the ground and casting their shade. It also occurs on the north side of a wall or fence. You will find it difficult to make a splash of colour unless you cover the ground in summer with Bizzie Lizzies, *Impatiens balsamina*. However, there are several plants with fine foliage, some evergreen, which will thrive. Ivies, hostas, lamium, periwinkle (*Vinca*), *Waldstenia ternata*, bergenias, *Symphitum grandiflorum* and Solomon's Seal (*Polygonatum grandiflorum*). You can get colour from hellebores, foxgloves, Dame's Violet (*Hesperis matronalis*), wood anemones, and the lovely fat pods opening to show off orange seeds of *Iris foetidissima*.

Colour in the Border

Is it presumptuous to think one has an eye for colour? Reading Gertrude Jekyll's *Colour in the Garden* makes me realize how slender my knowledge about it is. She writes of a blue garden, a green, a gold and a grey garden. Her thoughts about the colour garden may be transferred to bed or border, but in this case the surprise effect of walking from an enclosed area of one colour to the next will, of course, be wanting.

'How does one start? Miss Jekyll writes, 'Perhaps the Grey garden is seen at its best by reaching it through the orange borders.' Strong reds leading to orange and yellow will saturate the eye. It longs for the complementary colour, so that when you see the purple-blue and pink in the grey garden, 'the effect is surprisingly—astonishingly—luminous and refreshing.' The grey garden has plants with grey foliage, but the flowers can be white, pale pink, lilac and purple. There are no strong tones here and it is noticeable that many of the grey-leaf plants have lavender and pale pastel-coloured flowers.

The gold garden must follow next. Coming into it will be like stepping into sunshine. I have tried this, actually putting the gold planting in a shady part of the garden in order to bring light. It worked well then, but it is even more effective now that the elm trees which created the shade have died.

You pass from the yellow (or gold) to the blue garden. Your eye is filled with yellow influence, and 'no blue flower was ever so blue before'. Grey-blues may be used but not purple-blues such as the herbaceous lupin. Include creamy-whites, palest yellows and glaucous foliage. From the blue garden you should find yourself in the green garden where shrubs with polished leaves predominate. There are fewer flowers here and these should be white and pale yellow.

These thoughts serve as a model. They bring further ideas to the gardener's mind.

Notice that Miss Jekyll recommends that we should reach the grey garden through the orange *border*, not the orange garden, and that there is no mention of a red garden. A moderately large border, however, filled with hot reds and glowing orange can make a tremendous impact, so long as it is quite full. There is one special border I have in mind, at the Priory, Kemerton, near Tewkesbury. At the back are five shrubs with red leaves, *Cotinus coggyria* 'Notcutt's variety', two *Berberis* 'Atropurpurea', a red-leafed nut, and *Rosa rubrifolia*. In the middle ground are deep red roses, *Dahlia* 'Bishop of Llandaff' which has mahogany leaves as well as red flowers, *Lobelia cardinalis* 'Dark Crusader' mixed with the annual *Ricinus gibsonii* and bronze-leafed cannas. Red nicotianas and penstemon mix with fuchsias and monarda. Two other leaf textures are important, the Willow beet or 'ruby

Leaf colours are of immense importance in connection with flowers.

SHIRLEY HIBBERD 1884

Above: The spectacular borders in Mrs David Rockefeller's garden in Maine are planted to be at their peak for six weeks from mid-July. The strong colours of the annuals and hardy perennials are helped to vibrate by the inclusion of white flowers and grey foliage. The borders on the other side of this garden are planted with quieter, pastel shades.

Right: The white and grey border designed by Russell Page at the home of M. Bemburg, in France.

Top: *Clematis* 'Perle d'Azur'
and 'Madame Edouard André'
make a fine background for
richest blue monkshoods
(*aconitum*).

Middle: A cottage-garden medley
of mixed wallflowers, forget-me-
nots and ranunculus.

Bottom: Ornamental cabbage used
effectively beside fuschias and
Berberis darwinii 'Rose glow'.

Left: Part of a border designed
for pastel shades and leaf texture.
In the foreground is *Euphorbia
cyparisius*, contrasted with the
green spikes of hemerocallis and
the round, almost bronze leaves
of *Ligularia* 'Desdemona'.

chard', and tender coleus. Tall spikes of antholiza with their orange-red flowers give accents of green between the rounded clumps of sedum. In the front are large groupings of *Verbena* 'Lawrence Johnstone'. This border is startling and creates a feeling of joyous enthusiasm as one starts the journey about the garden. It is a border for July until the autumn, and, during those months, is a winner.

Gone are the days when many people had gardens large enough to have a spring border, a June border, annual beds (by these I do not mean bedding out in blocks of colour) and an autumn border. Most of us try to have consistent colour in the borders from spring until autumn. Obviously you cannot have a blaze of colour in every bed all this time, but the aim should be to have them looking interesting, with shapes and foliage and flowers starting in early spring.

We have a narrow border along a north-west-facing wall which gets a minimum of sun for half the year and only afternoon sun for the rest of it. By choosing spring flowers followed by climbers which bloom late, it is uninteresting only in December and January.

The *Helleborus orientalis* and *H. corsicus* are first on the scene, together with two sweet-smelling mahonias and an overhanging *Salix daphnoides aglaia*—a mass of silky plum catkins. We have tried crocuses here, but the mice living in the wall always make a meal of them. Next comes a succession of primroses and polyanthus which carry on well into May and by this time the early clematis are in full flower. So is *Ribes speciosum*, the fuchsia-flowered gooseberry with pendant red flowers. The lovely *Rosa* 'Mermaid' blooms early and climbs through *Hedera* 'Paddy's Pride', the yellow of the ivy leaf matching the rose. The long tassels of *Garrya elliptica* are now becoming brown and need removing and attention is focused on the old favourite *Rosa* 'Albertine'. A kolkwitzia, a deutzia and a *Buddleia alternifolia* are all treated as wall shrubs and later act as supports for August flowering clematis. The two I like best are *Clematis* x *Huldine* and *C.* 'Perle d'Azur', the latter growing through *Rosa rubrifolia*. *Itea ilicifolia* and *Buddleia fallowiana* 'Alba' now also come into bloom.

The easiest way to achieve colour in the borders in spring is to use bulbs. My habit is to plant the small *Iris reticulata* in the corners of the borders in the autumn, so we know where they are and can add to them. The crocuses, in theory, go down the middle, so their foliage is hidden by the leaves of emerging herbaceous plants, and I colonize them under deciduous shrubs. We treat scillas and pushkinianas in the same way. The daffodils are more difficult to conceal when their leaves are dying off, but I still like to have small drifts of them. You can plant them successfully through hardy geraniums and tough plants such as *Campanula glomerata*.

Tulips I treat quite differently. They are bedded out with forget-me-nots and sometimes with wallflowers. It is a regular autumn ritual and I have no compunction about spending money on them. I keep off parrot tulips, and doubles. It takes just one hard shower and they are spoilt. I love white tulips, especially the lily-flowered 'White Triumphator'; these associate well with the mixed pastel shades of wallflowers. A new discovery last spring was the triumph tulip 'Dreaming Maid' (the catalogue describes it as violet edged with white) which seems to be the perfect foil for forget-me-nots, as is the rose-coloured 'Marietta', a favourite of mine for many years.

Russell Page has been not only a good friend but also a constantly returning influence as I turn the pages of his book *The Education of a Gardener*. A photograph in this book of 'black and white tulips rising from a groundwork of blue forget-me-nots against a sunny white-washed wall' haunts me. I have no white wall so have put in darkest tulips, the Darwin 'Queen of Night', between *Ligularia* 'Desdemona' whose leaves as they emerge are purple and green. These dark tulips look spectacular growing through purple-leafed sage, in as large an area as you can spare.

All these bulbs may be left *in situ* except the bedded-out tulips, so you will be busy at the end of May lifting these and their forget-me-not and wallflower companions. Heel the tulips in an out-of-the-way place so that they can die down and be stored for another

In the management of the herbaceous border details are everything and principles next to nothing.

SHIRLEY HIBBERD 1884

year's display. Then you are left with those marvellous empty spaces where you can put summer-flowering annuals, the in-and-out bedding plants of despised Victorian gardens. I must admit that I do not choose lobelias, salvias and calceolarias with their blatant colours. I like love-in-the-mist, *Echium* 'Bluebedder', white nicotiana, pink agetum; these are all quiet colours which blend in with my perennial plants.

Other June-to-October contributors to our garden are the half-hardy 'Paris Daisy', *Chrysanthemum frutescens*, whose white flowers are incessantly in bloom, and (I wish I were more succesful with them) the sweet-smelling cherry pie, *Heliotrope peruvianum*. I especially appreciate the white tobacco plants—they have the best scent and look like ghosts standing out in the evening light. These annuals and half-hardies are support plants to the beds and borders where the perennials and shrubs play the most important parts. All make a long-lasting contribution.

Planning your border is like composing a menu. You have your main dish—the main feature plants in your border, and these have their accompaniments. The spring border will be light and fresh, the summer one more luscious and full, and the autumn border should leave you with a feeling of completion.

Over the years, I have discovered that the success or failure of my planting depends upon how much thought I have put into it and then have translated the thought into action. It has also proved essential to have standby plants to drop in where an idea has failed. Have a garden calendar if you have time, but be flexible and assess the situation as often as you can. What you put in you take out, be it aesthetic pleasure, vegetables, or cut flowers for the house.

CHAPTER SEVEN

THE WILD GARDEN AND MEADOW GARDENING

What more romantic way to spend an hour than sitting on a turf seat beside a flowery mead, with your lover beside you, his favourite greyhound at his feet and strains of music to beguile you? Many of the medieval illustrations give this idyllic impression. One of the best known, a fifteenth-century miniature in the Bibliothèque Nationale in Paris, has even more to tell. There is a fountain, a trellis-work fence to create an enclosure, two pots, one with carefully staked carnations and the other with a three-tiered evergreen, could it be a rosemary? Idyllic gardening scenes can be found in the backgrounds of many early pictures: Fra Angelico's fresco of the Annunciation in the Monastery of S.Marco Florence; Andrea del Verrocchio's *Annunciation* which hangs in the Uffizi Gallery also in Florence; the early sixteenth-century tapestry of the three Fates in the Victoria and Albert Museum, London; and many of Botticelli's pictures. These are but a few. Frequently, I have found myself unable to remember the foreground details of a picture, because when looking at it, my thoughts were concentrated on the background in which all sorts of ideas about early gardens are depicted. Although these features are often stylized renderings, they none the less represent the appearance of contemporary gardens. A constant feature is the delightful flowery mead often looking a bit tidier than it would have in reality. The orchards were the true pleasure gardens of these romantic times. In fact the manner in which wild flowers were allowed and probably encouraged to grow in them was a special feature.

Poets and writers help us imagine meads in gardens and orchards, too. Albertus Magnus, a monk who lived in the thirteenth century, says the orchard comprises primarily a grass plot of fine grass carefully weeded and trampled underfoot, a true carpet of green turf with no projections on its uniform surface. Petrus de Crescentius wrote about 1300 that the space cut off from the fields should be constantly weeded from worthless plants and the meadows should be mown twice a year to make them more beautiful. I believe he took the wild flowers for granted, he was so used to them. In the *Decameron*, Boccaccio describes a garden in the middle of which, more delightful than anything else, 'was a plot of ground like a meadow, the grass of a deep green, spangled with a thousand different flowers'. One wonders whether the owner, his friends and servants walked on these thousand flowers, crushing them, or picked their way carefully around them.

THE UNICORN TAPESTRIES

We are lucky in being able to identify many of the flowers in these meads by looking at old tapestries, some of which were so finely worked that species are recognizable. Everyone who has seen the Unicorn Tapestries donated by the late John D. Rockefeller to the Cloisters, New York, must have been amazed by their beauty: the fine workmanship, the dazzling white unicorn, the colours and tremendous variety of plants and trees which are so delicately and accurately stitched into the seven tapestries. But if we look into Margaret Freeman's book on them, we find not only the history of the tapestries but also the names of many of the plants. These were identified by members of the New York Botanic Garden (Carol Woodward and E.J. Alexander) and eighty-five of more than one hundred plants are so accurately embroidered that they are easily recognizable to a botanist. Plants are seen growing by a stream, in an orchard and a field, and in two of the tapestries they cover the entire background, so suggesting a flowery mead of the Middle Ages.

The background of the first tapestry, quite near the castle, where the hunters are setting off out of the orchard, is spangled with violets, the English daisy (*Bellis perennis*), the wild strawberry, periwinkles (*Vinca major* and *V. minor*) and daffodils. These all had a sym-

Opposite: The Unicorn in Captivity from The Hunt of the Unicorn in the Cloisters.

bolic or medical connotation. The violet is associated with the Virgin Mary for its humility—it has a place in love poetry too. In verses by John Lydgate, written to his lady on St. Valentine's Day, he entreats her 'O violet, fleur desiree... Since I am for you so amorous, embrace me, lady of the joyous heart.'

Chaucer wrote in his *Legend of Good Women*:

...of all the flowers in the mede

Then love I most these flowers white and red,

Such as men call daisies.

The wild strawberry often appears in medieval tapestries and paintings. In a Rhenish picture, the Virgin Mary sits on a bench covered with them, she has violets at her feet and a rose trellis behind her. The periwinkle, according to an early medical manuscript, has the unusual and useful virtue of curing discord between man and wife. Of the daffodil the same manuscript says, 'I know no flower like to it... thanks be to God it groweth in the mede.'

Among the other flowers that bloom in the Cloisters tapestry are marigolds, pimpernels, wallflowers and pansies, marguerites, primroses, yellow flag iris and *Iris germanica* (thought to be the fleur-de-lys in the arms of the French royal house), Chinese lanterns and wild orchids. In addition, there are English bluebells, bistort, cuckoo pint (*Arum maculatum*), carnations (*Dianthus caryophyllus*), at that time an emblem of betrothal and marriage, stock gilliflowers (*Matthiola incana*), columbines, a symbol of the Holy Spirit, and most beautiful of all, the Madonna lily, and in contrast, St Mary's thistle (*Silybum marianum*).

Most, but not all, of these plants are summer flowering—in fact they would have been in bloom before the grass grew too long and soon after they had faded the grass could be scythed to keep it strong and green.

THE DISAPPEARANCE OF THE FLOWERY MEADS

It was only later, when man began to be more sophisticated about his garden, that the lovely flowery meads were forgotten, nature was tamed, and topiary and careful cultivation became fashionable. But there is always a transitional period between the old and the new, for, as the saying goes, old habits die hard. And so we find that Francis Bacon, born in 1561, the nephew of Lord Burleigh, well-known for his gardening in his famous essay 'Of Gardens', thought that one third part of our garden plot should be 'framed as much as possible to a natural wildness'. The ground should be set with violets, strawberries and primroses. 'I like also little heaps, in the nature of mole-hills, to be set some with wild thyme...pinks, germander, periwinkle, cowslips, daisies, bear's foot and lily-of-the-valley. Bacon also liked to see standards of little bushes, such as roses, juniper, holly, red currants, gooseberries, rosemary, bay, sweet briar. 'These standards to be kept with cutting, that they grow not out of course.' It is worth a moment's thought to visualize this 'heath', as he calls it. Would there be grass growing between the periwinkle and thyme or would it be like a huge rock garden with several acres of ground cover? Bacon's selection of flowers is less varied than those pictured in the Unicorn tapestry, and he says, 'These are to be in the heath here and there, not in any order.' However much one may admire his masterly English, I do not believe that he was an experienced and very practical gardener. Even so his essay gives me immense pleasure, and presents a delightful vision of a meadow garden. But we must remember that Bacon was describing a garden of several acres and his heath was farthest from the house. The alleys, fountains and other ornaments, including a mount thirty feet high, were all set closer.

During the landscape movement in the eighteenth century, the equivalent of the flowery meadow or meadow garden would have been the effect created by the introduction of the ha ha. The meadow would not have been so flowery but would have had grazing cattle, sheep and sometimes picturesque deer roaming the parkland. The wild flowers in these parks were unintentional. Every field and hedgerow teemed with wild plants in

'My flowers grow up in several parts of the garden in the greatest luxuriancy and profusion. I am so far from being fond of any particular one, by reason of its rarity, that if I meet with any one in a field which pleases me, I give it a place in my garden. By this means, when a stranger walks with me he is surprised to see several large spots of ground covered with ten thousand different colours...'

JOSEPH ADDISON, 1712.

the age before agricultural spraying. There can never have been a time when a gardener somewhere did not enjoy encouraging meadow flowers at the edge of his garden. But for years increasingly specialized and exotic plants were cultivated. We can understand the heights this reached when we read William Robinson's attempts to coax Victorian gardeners from thinking that their tender plants often in garish colours, bedded out and carpet bedded, were the most splendid things they could grow. It was not their fault. They were living at a time when all sorts of exotic plants were being introduced into England, such as lobelias, calceolarias and pelargoniums. This was combined with the recent mushrooming of glass houses of all shapes and sizes thirty years before—a direct result of the removal of the tax on glass and the invention of sheet glass. All the plants grown in the glass house, many of them because they were a novelty, were bedded out somewhere in the garden and, to make room for them, the tried old hardy favourites were cast out and became Cinderellas of the garden. These are the plants we now call 'cottage-garden plants' and use for our herbaceous borders. William Robinson described this change as the 'rooting out of all the old favourites', and added that it was not uncommon to find the largest gardens in the country without a single hardy flower, all energies being devoted to the few exotics for the summer decoration.

The Wild Garden

Robinson wrote a wonderful book called *The Wild Garden* and said that he wanted to show 'how we may have more of the varied beauty of hardy flowers than the most ardent admirer of the old style of gardening ever dreams of, by naturalizing many beautiful plants in our fields, outer parts of our pleasure grounds and in neglected places in almost every kind of garden...They are the lilies, and bluebells, and foxgloves, and irises, and windflowers, and columbines, and violets, and crane's-bills, and countless pea-flowers, and moon daisies, and brambles, and cinquefoils, and evening primroses, and clematis, and honeysuckles, and michaelmas daisies, and bindweeds, and forget-me-nots, and blue omphalodes, and primroses, and day lilies, and asphodels, and myriads of plants which form the flora of the northern or temperate regions of vast continents.' I make no excuse for quoting William Robinson and listing the flowers he suggests. His book caused quite a stir and those Victorian ladies who loved nature must surely have been delighted to be encouraged to grow the 'wild' flowers that they had admired on their nature and botany walks. Every one of his suggestions looks well in today's wild garden.

Understand, though, that William Robinson was not encouraging a return to flowery meads. 'Some have mistaken the idea of the wild garden,' he wrote, 'as a plan to get rid of all formality near the house; whereas it will restore to its true use the flower-garden, now subjected to two tearings up a year—i.e. in spring and autumn... Spring flowers are easily grown in multitudes away from the house, and therefore for their sakes the system of digging up the flower-beds twice a year need not be carried out.' The essential beds round the house should be constantly cleared and infilled in order to keep them looking well-tutored and interesting all the time, but the wild garden is quite different. Here plants should be allowed to seed themselves and grow in an unhampered, natural manner, under the trees or through the grass.

There has been some misunderstanding as to the term 'Wild Garden'. It is applied essentially to the placing of perfectly hardy exotic plants under conditions where they will thrive without further care.

WILLIAM ROBINSON 1894

Practical Wild Gardening

Spring-flowering bulbs are the earliest joy, growing in grass, along with the primroses. Winter aconites, *Eranthis hyemalis*, together with snowdrops, appear first. They are followed by anemones, scillas and crocuses. The leaves of these soon die down and all of them will seed themselves freely if given the chance to do so. I have discovered that the surest time to divide snowdrops and aconites is as their flowers fade, in fact while they are 'in the green'.

Solomon's Seal, *Polygonatum multiflorum*.

The whole success of wild gardening depends on arranging bold, natural groups with a free hand.

WILLIAM ROBINSON 1894

The advantage of doing so then is that you can see exactly where more drifts are needed.

Daffodils have long been thought the most important of all these early flowers. William Robinson thought so too, and one can but agree with him. They are a special feature of many spring gardens both for their scent and promise of spring. Great drifts of daffodils were planted in the 'wilderness' in our garden, long years before I ever came to live here. Every April we look forward to them with anticipation and for at least four weeks they make a golden display.

They were planted long before we added the ornamental trees and now I often wish they had been put in drifts of the same varieties to make a more organized effect, with great swathes of one colour. A counsel of perfection is to give the leaves a spraying of liquid fertilizer when they are at their greenest and not to cut leaves until six weeks after the peak of perfection of the flowers. We have kept to the latter rule for the past decade and it has not failed us or the daffodils. But if you are aiming at a true flower meadow, then June is much too soon for the first cut; you should wait until July for the other flower seeds to ripen.

William Robinson's suggestions for suitable flowers include Solomon's Seal (*Polygonatum multiflorum*), 'arching forth from a shady recess behind tufts of daffodils' and I would add in front of a later flowering shrub such as budleia or deutzia, or an evergreen escallonia or osmanthus both of whose small shiny leaves would contrast well with the Solomon's Seals.

PLANTING IN GRASS

This needs a different technique from planting in a border. Each variety should grow in natural groups with the odd one or two straying out and merging into its neighbour. If they are allowed to seed themselves this effect will happen naturally. *Anemone apennina* and *A. nemerosa*, grape hyacinths (*Muscari*), snowdrops, chionodoxas and many of the crocuses will thrive in grassland and flower well before the grass becomes too tall. The hybrid *Erythronium* 'Pagoda', once established, is very free-flowering and likes to be under deciduous trees so it has full sun in spring and is slightly shaded later. Our best patch is under a weeping cherry but the same effect could be created by using them on the north side of a shrub. The prettily mottled leaves and flowers always cause comment. Snakeshead fritillaries are among the most satisfactory meadow flowers; they stand up so well above the grass and will spread fast once they become established.

The Edge of the Wood

The flowery mead and the wild garden are two distinct features for your garden. The meadow flowers of the flowery mead grow intermingled, forming a delicate, multicoloured tapestry amongst the grasses. The plants in the wild garden are planned in drifts around free-standing trees, perhaps on the edge of woodland. It is this edge of the wild garden I want to turn to now. Here there is a variety of opportunity, with different situations, some in shade and others in full sun most of the day but sheltered from north winds. I know a lovely nut walk at the top of a cottage garden where in spring, as the nut catkins come into prominence a host of amazing hellebores are at their best, mingled with snowdrops. These are *Helleborus orientalis* in a range of colours from white through pink to deep maroony red. Turn up their faces and many of them have delicate darker flakes. If you buy the named varieties they will cost you a lot of money, but with patience you can build up your own stock from a few plants. This is what I did and now we have a fine show in a wide colour range. Take care not to weed out the seedlings, though you should dig up a few of them where they have seeded in profusion, and put them into trays. Keep these in the frame for a few months until their second pair of leaves appear and then you can plant them back into the garden. I do the same with the tiny hardy cyclamen which seed beside their parents. We gather these as they germinate in spring, put them in trays and keep them safe until they are large enough to care for themselves in the garden. Older, larger corms are able to fend for themselves in grass under trees, but the small corms must be given more consideration in order to survive. Gertrude Jekyll is especially good at describing the plants which help the wild garden to merge into the woodland. We have become so accustomed to wanting the best, most scented varieties of mahonia, that we are apt to overlook the more humble *M. aquifolium*. It is a tough, attractive, useful form of ground cover, at its best in mid-winter when its leaves are a lovely tawny red. Then as spring advances the yellow flowers attract the early bees.

With an acid soil every garden owner wants rhododendrons and azaleas. These must be planted at a distance to allow for their ultimate spread—so the spaces between must be temporarily filled. Jekyll's recommendations are heaths and andromeda, ferns and *Cistus laurifolius*. The latter is short-lived and so it will succumb by the time the rhododendrons have joined hands. Lilies thrive in good shady soil and love to push their way through shrubs. *Lilium Auratum* flowers in late summer and enjoys a peat soil, so it is the ideal lily for an acid soil. From years ago, when I first started to garden, I have a vivid memory of sitting on a garden bench and behind me was a thicket of *Senecio* 'Sunshine' through which were growing a mass of *Lilium* 'Henryii' (both lime-tolerant so an idea for my own garden).

Lilium Auratum.

CLIMBERS

Climbing roses and those autumn-flowering clematis make perfect companions for evergreen yew, holly and box. You must take care that the climber is not too vigorous or perchance it will harm the evergreen. For this reason I choose the autumn clematis, for it demands hard pruning in spring; *Clematis flammula*; the beautiful *C. texensis* varieties; *C.* 'Duchess of Albany'; *C.* 'Gravetye Beauty', one of my great favourites, it should be grown through a sturdy bush of *Rosa rubrifolia*; and *Clematis* 'Étoile Rose', perhaps one of the most desirable of all clematis. Many of the taller plants which self sow are suitable for the edge of the wild garden where it joins woodland or meets a boundary fence or hedge. Digitalis and mulliens (verbascums) are good examples and both so easy. It is wise only to allow flowers with the best colours to ripen their seeds. If you prefer white foxgloves, then gather and scatter their seed liberally and rogue out the duller purple specimens to prevent them seeding. The same thing applies to verbascums which vary in quality of leaf texture; my preference is for the cream-coloured flowers. Angelica and fennel are two more which look well against a background of trees. The feathery leaves of sweet cicely (*Myrrhis odoratus*) contrast well with dark green holly.

Clematis 'Etoile Rose'.

Left: A fine stand of the giant hogweed (*Heracleum giganteum*) backed by an old box bush. The hogweed takes one summer to attain its height; the box takes decades.

An experiment I intend to try one summer is to make use of the tall stems, sometimes as high as 12 ft (3.65 m) of *Heracleum giganteum*, the giant hogweed. By mid-July their seed heads must be cut off or you will have a veritable forest of them in a few years. I know a High Court judge who sold his house because of his hogweed forest. The golden hop, *Humulus Lupulus* 'Aureus', is a perennial climber which make yards of growth each summer. It is too weighty to be allowed to grow through a dark green holly box bush or the like so we have planted it at the feet of the heracleum. We will take off the seed head and allow the hop to drape itself round the hogweed's prickly stem. Another such coat-hanger effect could be achieved using the skeleton stems of *Crambe cordifolia*, whose flowers are over by mid-July, combining it with an autumn clematis which is pruned hard: *Clematis tangutica* would be good. To quote Gertrude Jekyll again: 'Wild gardening is a delightful, and in good hands a most desirable pursuit, but no kind of gardening is so difficult to do well...Because it has in some measure become fashionable, and because it is understood to mean the planting of exotics in wild places, unthinking people rush to the conclusion that they can put any garden plant into any wild places, and that that is wild gardening. I have seen woody places that were already perfect with their own simple charm just muddled and spoilt by a reckless planting of garden refuse.' So beware.

The golden hop (*Humulus lupulus*) makes tremendous annual growth. It can be used to create a summer covering for an old tree trunk or an arbour.

The meadow garden at Great Dixter in April with snakeshead fritillaries and naturalized primulas. The meadow must be left uncut until the seeds of these flowers have ripened and dispersed.

Although this was written in 1899, wild gardening is still fashionable and the idea of meadow gardening is becoming widely appreciated. Any gardener who has visited Christopher Lloyd's garden at Great Dixter and seen his beautiful meadow garden between spring and mid-July will have been impressed by the marvellous variety of flowers standing out boldly in the grass. He has written: 'Gardening in a meadow is a relaxed pursuit. There are no obligatory planting programmes or deadlines; you can do as little or as much of this as suits your inclination.' Comforting words from one of our most illustrious gardeners. To read in full what he has said you can find two articles in the June and July 1976 numbers of *The Garden*, the journal of the Royal Horticultural Society.

I hope the reader may now be intrigued by the thought of doing as little as he pleases. Here are some practical thoughts as to how you may achieve a modern flowery mead put together for me by another expert on the subject, Chris Baines.

Practical Meadow Gardening

The natural habitat for many of our prettiest and most colourful flowers is grassland. We modern gardeners spend a great deal of our time struggling to keep grasses out of the flower borders, and 'weeds' out of the lawn. Meadow gardening provides an ideal opportunity for us to relax a little, and work in harmony with nature, rather than in conflict. If you have a soft spot for dreamy, wild-flower meadows, the flowery meads of mediaeval days sprinkled with buttercups and humming with the summer buzz of insects may capture a little of that romance even in the smallest of gardens.

In garden-design terms it is easiest to think of your 'meadow' simply as a lawn of a different texture. Be positive about its shape and establish a 'crisp' line where the meadow meets your manicured lawn. In larger gardens, use this 'rougher' style of grassland to soften the transition from formal terrace and flower bed to informal orchard, shrubbery or copse. If you have trees which interfere with mowing and cast a shade which spoils the quality of your lawn, change the area into wood-meadow, and your troubles will disappear, and give your garden a new feature.

SOIL, PLANTS AND MANAGEMENT

There are three factors which influence the character of a meadow: physical circumstances, available plants and the pattern of your management. A rich, fertile soil will favour coarse grasses and a small range of vigorous, tall, broadleaves. Poor soil will restrict the grass growth and encourage far more of the colourful flowers to compete. A sandy soil will have a different flora from a heavy clay, and of course pH will also have an effect. Some flowers thrive beneath the shade of trees; others need full sunshine, and a north-facing slope will support a plant community different from one which slopes to the south.

Probably you are stuck with a particular set of physical and climatic circumstances and must make do with the flowers that suit best. Occasionally, though, there is an opportunity for change—you could improve drainage, for instance, or even create mounds which will give you a variety of aspects.

'The second major influence is the type of plants which will thrive on your soil. The seed of some meadow flowers is very mobile. Many of the common 'daisy' types of flower have fluffy seed heads which can drift for miles. Others are much more sedentary, relying on the odd gust of wind, or perhaps a passing ant to transport seed just a few feet. The seeds of primroses, for example, have a waxy coating which ants apparently find delicious. They steal the seed when it is ripe, carry it away, strip off the wax and abandon the seed, leaving it to germinate where it will not compete with the parent plant. It is tempting to think that if you simply stop mowing your lawn, a whole tapestry of rare and beautiful wild flowers will spring into life, but unless you are very lucky, the natural seed bank will be fairly limited and you will need to introduce the more exotic species.

The third influence is management. The 'natural' wild flower meadows we treasure most all share one characteristic. Without exception they have been managed on a regular, unchanging pattern for many, many years. North Meadow, for instance, the national nature reserve near Cricklade, on the Thames, is famous for its millions of beautiful *Fritillaria meleagris* every spring. The fritillaries, white and checkered purple, flower in May, and their seed is ripe by late June. If the meadow were mown or grazed in early summer, then quite obviously the fritillaries would be unable to complete their life cycle, and they would quickly disappear. In fact, North Meadow is a 'lammas meadow' cut for hay in late July by when the seeds have ripened and fallen, as they have done for the past several hundred years. This particular mowing regime allows the fritillaries, cowslips and several other pretty spring flowers to thrive and multiply. From September until February, cattle graze the

Opposite: **Beautiful English woodland with a carpet of bluest bluebells (*Endymion nonscriptus*). It was of this sort of scene that Gertrude Jekyll wrote 'I have seen woody places that were already perfect with their own simple charm just muddled and spoilt by a reckless planting of garden refuse'.**

Snake's head fritillary (*Fritillaria meleagris*).

wet meadow, cropping the 'aftermath' and so constraining late-summer flowering plants which might otherwise out-compete those of spring. The cattle also serve to break up the turf a little each year, and so provide the gaps in which fresh seed can germinate.

The trampling of cattle may not be your idea of sound garden husbandry, but certainly it is vital that the garden meadow has a regular cropping pattern of some sort if its wild flowers are to survive and multiply.

Before moving on to make practical recommendations about meadow gardening, I think it is important to dispel one common myth. Many people talk of poppy meadows, and no such thing exists. Poppies, mayweed and heart's-ease are all very beautiful, very colourful wild flowers, but they are not meadow flowers. The bright blue cornflower and the magenta corncockle give the game away. These are all wild flowers of the cornfields; they spring up annually, their seeds having been brought to the surface by cultivation. They do not live on and they cannot compete with mown grass sward. Certainly there should be a place for them in the garden, but they must be grown as annuals, just like candytuft, clarkia and calendula. They can only survive in disturbed soil, although it is true that poppies in particular can survive as dormant seed for decades, and you may well find them mixed in with your other seedlings in the first year or two of a newly sown lawn or meadow.

Converting an Established Lawn

Provided cowslips (*Primula veris*) (*top*) and the rarer oxlip (*Primula elatior*) (*bottom*) are allowed to flower, set and drop seeds they will increase in number.

Primula elatior.

The more starved and weedy your existing lawn is, the better off you are. This kind of lawn—an embarrassment for years—should be redefined as a rich tapestry of fine, poverty-resistant grasses such as bents and fescues, and flattened star-shaped rosette plants. Simply give the 'weeds' a chance to flower and you will be amazed at the beauty of some of these suppressed wild flowers. Alternatively, if your lawn is vigorous, bright green and weed-free, then it may take several years to develop that exhausted condition which favours colourful flowers.

As a first step towards meadow gardening, try simply raising the blades of your mower to about 2 in (5 cm). This enables you to maintain your weekly cut and keep the lawn looking very tidy, but at the same time it does allow quite a range of low-growing meadow flowers to thrive. If you take off the clippings each time you mow, then the colourful flowers will multiply as the fertility drops.

The next step, perhaps after a year or two of enjoying a neat carpet of bugle (*Ajuga reptans*), speedwell (*Veronica chamaedrys*) and stitchwort (*Stellaria graminea*), is to introduce a gap of four or five weeks into your normal mowing regime. Many of the more common lawn weeds can flower over a long period in the summer. If you stop mowing for a month or so at any time from May to September you are likely to unlock a colourful display of rosette plants such as hoary plantain (*Plantago media*), Cat's-ear (*Hypochoeris radicata*) and of course the ubiquitous daisy (*Bellis perennis*). Give these flowers a chance to bloom and seed each year, and their numbers will quickly build up. Other meadow flowers are not qute so co-operative. You may have the odd cowslip lurking in your lawn, for example. Cowslips flower in May/June and unless you have your break in the mowing pattern at around that time of year, the cowslips will never flower, and so will gradually disappear. Many other meadow flowers are equally choosy, and that of course makes them very susceptible to changes in agricultural practice. This helps to explain why so many of them are becoming rare in the countryside.

VARIED MOWING PATTERNS

If you have the room, then it is well worth adopting more than one pattern of mowing regime, and this will increase the range of flowers you encourage. Leave one patch of 'meadow' until June before cutting it for the first time, and then cut it regularly for the rest of the summer. This will favour primroses (*Primula vulgaris*) and snowdrops (*Galan-*

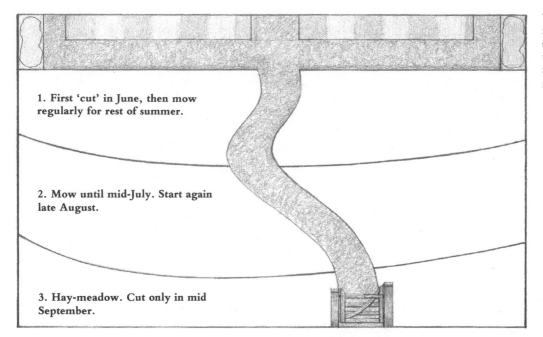

Three different mowing patterns for a meadow garden. In each case the mown grass must be removed to reduce fertility, thus favouring flowers rather than coarse-growing grasses.

1. First 'cut' in June, then mow regularly for rest of summer.

2. Mow until mid-July. Start again late August.

3. Hay-meadow. Cut only in mid September.

thus nivalis). Mow a second area through the early spring, stop for a month or so in high summer, and then start cutting again in late August. A whole range of meadow plants will provide a colourful display about 18 in (45 cm) tall, and many of the beautiful fine grasses will flower too.

A third area, perhaps rather further from the house, might be managed for tall hay-meadow species. Such beautiful wild flowers as field scabious (*Knautia arvensis*), knapweed (*Centaurea scabiosa*) and lady's bedstraw (*Galium verum*) will all thrive under this regime, which also provides an invaluable habitat for many butterflies and other attractive creatures. Cut the hay in mid-September, and rake it off before the autumn wet weather sets in.

Whichever mowing regime you choose, it is vital that the clippings (or the hay) are removed. In this way the fertility is constantly reduced and the flowers are favoured rather than the coarse grasses. Leave the cut grass to rot down and you will very quickly produce a jungle of coarse growth, and the beauty of the meadow will be spoilt.

Above top: Field Scabious (*Knautia arvensis*).

Above bottom: Lady's bedstraw (*Galium verum*).
Hay-meadow species such as these will flower if the meadow garden is not cut until mid-September.

Left: Greater knapweed (*Centaurea scabiosa*)

Introducing New Plants

There are very few established lawns which are completely free of 'weeds', so a change of regime is almost certain to give you some meadow-flower colour. It seems likely, however, that you will want to increase the range, and once you have selected a particular regime, that becomes relatively simple. Bulbs and corms are the easiest to introduce of course— they are so conveniently packaged. If you fancy waves of daffodils, sheets of crocuses or clumps of dog's-tooth violet (*Erythronium dens-canis*), choose a patch of meadow which remains uncut until June, scatter the bulbs and plant them where they fall. The spring meadow will allow their foliage to die back after flowering, and so build up the food-store for the

A Cornish meadow covered with lesser celandines (*Ranunculus ficaria*), primroses (*Primula vulgaris*) and wild dog-violets (*Viola riviniana*).

following spring's display. If you have a summer meadow, you might like to try the summer-flowering Martagon lilies (*Martagon lilium*) or perhaps the summer hyacinth (*Gaultonia candicans*), the tiger flower (*Trigridia pavonia*) or the good old montbretia (*Crocosmia crocosmiiflora*). We tend to think mainly of spring bulbs for 'naturalizing' but there really are some wonderful summer bulbs to experiment with, too. Choosing bulbs for your particular mowing scheme is quite simple if you consider their flowering time. One word of warning, mice are very partial to snippings of the early bulbs, especially crocus.

It is a little more difficult to introduce herbaceous perennials into an established meadow. If you choose to employ seeds then they need a gap in the sward if they are to germinate and establish successfully. These do occur naturally, on a small scale with wormcasts for example, or on a rather more dramatic scale with molehills, but if you want to be fairly sure of some success, it is better to make your own gaps. On relatively young grassland you may succeed simply by scarifying the turf with a wire rake at the time of sowing. If, however, you are dealing with a long established grassland, then you will have better luck if you either strip off small patches of turf to reveal the soil below, or else use a selective weedkiller to remove some of the competition. With formal lawns you would use a herbicide which kills broad-leaved weeds and leaves grasses unscathed. In meadow gardening you are aiming at the opposite effect. Choose a herbicide which selectively kills monocotyledons, and water on the weakest recommended concentration, taking great care to avoid any contamination of areas which have bulb foliage still visible. (Monocotyledons are narrow-leaved plants and include such things as snowdrops, daffodils and lilies as well as grasses.)

If used with care and sensitivity, these selective herbicides can be extremely valuable. By knocking back the grasses, the broad-leaved plants are given a boost, and certainly it is worth experimenting with this as a method of increasing the population of existing meadow flowers, as well as providing space for the germination of newly sown seed.

Even if you do create spaces in the sward, oversowing is a fairly haphazard way of introducing new species. It is far better to grow the plants you want as individuals, in just the same way as you would produce bedding or border plants. Grow the seedlings on in small pots or in a prepared seed bed, and when they are well-formed plants, transplant them into the meadow. Plant out each species in drifts, grouping several plants together. In this way they are more likely to look 'natural' and to begin to cross-fertilize and establish a worthwhile colony.

Brand New Meadows

Starting a meadow from scratch is easier in many ways. You have greater control over the plant species, and the techniques are more akin to 'normal' gardening.

Obviously some kind of meadow can be produced on almost any soil, but if you have a choice, then well-drained, nutrient-poor soil will give you the most colourful results. If you are faced with a rich top soil, then think of removing a few inches of it. Its high fertility will no doubt prove useful for vegetables or some more orthodox garden feature such as a shrubbery or a herbaceous border. Poverty is the key to meadow-gardening success.

If you are actually importing soil to a new garden, then try to acquire some sandy sub soil for the meadow area and if you are involved in this degree of upheaval, then it is certainly worth putting in a simple land drainage scheme if the site is wet. Wet meadows do exist of course, and in fact they provide a habitat for some of the most beautiful wild flowers—meadowsweet (*Filipendula ulmaria*), purple loosestrife (*Lythrum salicaria*), ragged-robin (Lychnis flos-cuculi) and marsh marigold (*Caltha palustris*), for example. You must remember, however, that in the countryside these wet-meadow communities are generally grazed rather than mown, and that makes them far more difficult to translate into the garden context.

Once you have selected your site, cultivate the soil as normal to provide a fine, firm seed bed. Most of the seed you will be sowing is very fine indeed, and this means that your seed bed preparation is even more critical than usual.

Ideally, meadow sowing should take place in late summer. This is the natural season for meadow flowers to shed their seed. However, there may be circumstances when you wish to sow in the spring. This is quite possible, though the disadvantage is that many young wild flower seeds are only viable for a short period, and when sown in the late summer or early autumn will germinate more readily and at a higher percentage than if they are kept in an envelope and sown in the spring. Try to prepare the soil a month or two in

Opposite: **Lobelia cardinalis** is more suitable for a herbaceous border or damp garden in England, but in North Carolina and other parts of America where it grows wild in wooded areas it makes a spectacular addition to a wild garden scene.

LOBELIA
CARDINALIS
N. AMERICA.

advance of sowing as this will give the 'weeds' which already exist in the soil a chance to re-emerge. The annual weeds of cultivation are of little consequence, since they will quickly succumb to mowing, but this rest period does give you the chance to deal with the more troublesome perennials. There are a number of unwanted species which will grow quite happily amidst the competition of a meadow sward, and these are easier to eradicate before seed sowing than after. Small fragments of such plants as couch grass (*Agropyron repens*), creeping thistle (*Cirsium arvense*) and dock (*Rumex obtusifolius*) will push up vigorous new shoots within a week or so of cultivation, and again herbicides can be used to eliminate them. This time a non-selective, systemic, contact, non-residual weedkiller should be used, either as a simple over-spray, or in gel form applied directly to the offending new shoots. The herbicide will travel in through the green leaves, and be translocated down into the root system, killing the plant completely. Since the chemical is non-residual, the seed-bed can be safely sown at any time after spraying.

SOWING

The sowing rates for wild-flower meadows are extremely light. This is partly because most of the seeds are very fine, and consequently there are a great many individuals to the gram, and partly because the individual seedlings are particularly susceptible to overcrowding. Such small quantities of fine seeds are notoriously difficult to sow evenly, and you will find sowing much easier by bulking up the seed with clean sawdust or silver sand. The seed must always be very thoroughly mixed to give an even coverage of all the species, and the light colour of the sawdust helps enormously when trying to sow evenly by hand. The mixture shows up clearly against the dark soil. The seed mixture really need not be very complicated. The main rule is to avoid vigorous grass species. A normal lawn mixture 'without ryegrass' will provide an excellent basis for most situations, though several seed houses sell selected mixtures of grasses for wet soils, dry, acid, or alkaline soils. The key species to look for are the bents (*Agrostis* species) and fescues (*Festuca* species), and if you are planning a summer hay meadow, then grass species such as sweet vernal (*Anthoxanthum odoratum*) and timothy (*Phleum pratensis*) are worth including in small quantities. These are the grasses whose seed heads look so pretty waving in the wind. So far as the meadow flowers themselves are concerned, it is probably easiest to sow a ready-prepared mixture. A growing number of seedsmen are marketing a wild-flower mix, and whilst these will generally contain a wide range of species, suited to a variety of conditions, your soil and the subsquent mowing regime will quickly favour appropriate types, and eliminate others. If you want lots of colour in the first year or two then by all means include a few annual 'weeds of cultivation'—either British natives such as poppy (*Papaver rhoeas*) and cornflower (*Centauria cyanus*) or perhaps spectacular exotics such as Californian poppy (*Eschscholtzia spp*) and Virginia stock. They will have dropped out long before they can become a nuisance.

There is a tendency to think of meadows as exclusively wild-flower communities, but there is a wide range of meadow plants from other countries. Many of these are available as individually packeted seed, and if they are hardy perennials, then they too can be introduced at the sowing stage. The effect can be a little startling, however, when the result is an English meadow full of gaillardias, michaelmas daisies and golden rod, as surprising but less natural to me as my first glimpse of wild asters in New England, *Lobelia cardinalis* in North Carolina and the beautiful butterfly weed, growing in natural profusion in New Jersey. There are the sights which the plant hunters saw and marvelled at, before sending home the seeds for English herbaceous borders.

WILDLIFE

There is one extremely important reason for sticking mainly to native plants, whatever country you live in. A particularly delightful feature of garden meadows is the attractive

Left: **Sweet vernal grass
(*Anthoxanthum odoratum*).**

Right: **Timothy grass (*Phleum
pratense*). Both these grasses look
pretty in the summer hay meadow
and make unusual dried
decorations.**

wildlife they can support. The insect life is fascinating, with many species of butterflies, of course, but with grasshoppers, brightly coloured beetles and hoverflies, honeybees and bumbles too. This invertebrate community in turn provides the food for many species of predators, from shrews and lizards to owls and falcons, and the whole complex and sometimes spectacular food web begins with plants. Native animals depend fundamentally on native plants. Many of the butterflies, for example, may well be able to thrive as adults by feeding on the nectar of a huge range of exotic species, but their caterpillars will all, without exception, be strictly limited in their diet to just one or two food species. The meadow is a place where some of these food plants can grow. The small copper butterfly, for instance, often feeds as an adult on buddleia, but its larvae can only feed on one or two species of sorrel, dock and knotgrass. Meadow brown is a real feature of a summer meadow garden, and its larval food is restricted to just one or two of the meadow grasses. The common blue, a particularly brilliant creature, must have the leaves of either black medic (*Medicago lupulina*) or bird's-foot-trefoil (*Lotus corniculatus*) to complete its life-cycle, and both species are included in most meadow flower seed mixtures. A study of the relationship between plant and insect life is a fascinating subject which can open up whole new vistas and is a marvellous way to interest children to the natural world about them.

LATE SOWING

A late-summer sowing should give you a 'green sheen' of germinated seedlings within a couple of weeks. Not all of the species will germinate immediately. Some will need the triggering stimulus of winter frosts before germinating the following spring. Generally,

though, there should be a good even covering before the winter, and a sowing rate of, say, 3/16 oz (5 gm) of grass seed and 4 drams (0.5 gm) of wild-flower seed per square yard should minimize the risk of any damping off caused through overcrowding.

It is important to mow the young seedlings when they reach a height of about 4 in (10 cm). Set the mower blades as high as possible—3 in (7 cm) if you can. Make sure that the machine is sharp, to avoid pulling the seedlings up, and simply slice off the tops. This will stimulate 'tillering' or basal growth in the grasses, and the broad-leaved seedlings will be made sturdier, too.

From then on it is plain sailing. You will probably need to mow three or four times in the first season, remembering to rake off the clippings, and never to set the blades lower than 2 in (5 cm). By the second summer you should be able to settle into your regular regime, and treat the new lawn in much the same way as was advocated earlier. There may be a few rogue coarse weeds which re-emerge to tower above the rest. These should be few and far between and can usually be carefully removed by hand. If there are too many for that approach, then use a gel-based contact, systemic herbicide, and simply paint it on to the leaves of the offending plants. They will gradually wither away.

SEED COLLECTING

My assumption so far has been that you will buy seed from a seedsman. Certainly that is a sensible policy for large quantities, and particularly for the grasses. There is, however, something very attractive about the idea of stocking a meadow with plants from other familiar places. Whilst it is irresponsible and, in Britain at least, illegal, to dig up wild plants, all but the most rare and precious of them can be introduced as seed. In my own sandy meadow we have a colony of sheep's-bit scabious collected as seed on a late summer holiday in Ireland. They are extremely beautiful in their own right, but they provide an extra thrill of nostalgia each time they flower, simply because of their pedigree. Seed collection is really very straightforward. Collect the flower heads when they are almost ripe, invert them into a paper bag, and the seed will fall out as they ripen. Do not store them in polythene bags. Generally speaking, seeds need to breathe, until they are ripe. Try to sow as soon as possible. Most seed is best sown fresh, though of course it may not necessarily germinate immediately. Some seed will last for years in storage, and deteriorate very little, but as a general rule, immediate sowing is safest, and some species—notably cowslips (*Primula veris*)—germinate much more successfully if sown in their first season.

Of course a grassland community is more than a simple collection of plants. We have already thought about the excitement of the animal life, and whilst the more mobile species will find your meadow surprisingly quickly, the rich complex of soil organisms and mini-beasts which complete the picture are obviously far less capable of 'dropping in'. For this reason it is worth introducing just a few turves into your lawn.

Although it is obviously wrong to raid the rich meadows of the countryside, there may be friends with 'weedy lawns' who can donate a square foot or two to your new meadow. Regrettably, too, there is, even now, a relentless preoccupation with building on green fields around every town and city, and a phone call to the local nature conservation society will almost certainly lead you to an exciting meadow somewhere in your locality, soon to be destroyed, and therefore ideal as a donor of a small nugget of meadow-history.

Britain has lost ninety-five per cent of its species-rich wild-flower meadows in the past forty years. In just two generations the common wild flowers and butterflies of childhood have become rarities. Meadow-gardening can provide some real compensation for all that destruction. Some of the more precious plants have gone for ever, of course, but many of the survivors could be given sanctuary in our gardens, and by creating a network of mini-meadows in our towns and villages, we will be providing great pleasure for ourselves, and securing a little of the romance and beauty of flower meadows for future generations too.

Opposite: Ox-eye daisies (*Chrysanthemum leucathemum*) buttercups (*Ranunculus bulbosus*) and hawkweed (*Trieracium*). Britain has lost ninety-five per cent of its species-rich wild-flower meadows such as this in the last forty years.

CHAPTER EIGHT
Topiary

Trees and shrubs clipped into different shapes can create a powerful effect in any garden. My preference is for neat hedges and geometrical shapes rather than artificial animals and birds, for in the long run they tend not only to have the most impact but also harmonize better with other features in the garden. And though few people would consider devoting their entire garden to a topiary display such as that at Levens Hall in Cumbria (even if it was within their ability), everyone should consider including the satisfying lines of a neatly clipped yew or hornbeam hedge.

Origins

We do not know who first used shears to clip their trees into fantastic shapes of carved vegetation, but like most ideas and fashions it probably evolved slowly. Illustrations of an Egyptian garden in about 1400 BC show lines of date and doum palms creating the symmetry of the garden. The date palms appear shaped in perfect cones on single trunks, a fine array of tonsored trees, or is this a stylized picture of their natural form? We know that when Caesar returned to Rome from Egypt the practice of clipping bushes was becoming increasingly fashionable, which leads one to assume that the Romans not only learnt the art from the Egyptians but were sufficiently impressed by its effects to wish to have clipped trees in their own gardens.

According to Columella, it was Caesar's contemporary Cnais Matius who first practised the art. Garden design, Cicero mentions, was the work of the *toparius*, but Pliny never uses this word although he writes fully on the work in his own formal garden, calling the designer the artificer (*artifax*). It was later that the phrase *opus topiarii* became associated with the clipping of evergreens.

PLINY

Pliny's letter to Apollinaris gives a clear description of his garden in Tuscany.
'In front of the portico is a terrace divided into a great number of geometrical figures, and abounded with a box hedge. The descent from the terrace is a sloping bank, adorned with a double row of box trees cut in the shapes of animals; the level ground at the foot of the bank is covered with the soft, I had almost said liquid, acanthus. This lawn is surrounded by a wall enclosed with dense evergreens, trimmed into a variety of forms. Beyond is an *allée* laid out in the form of a circus, which encircles a plantation of box trees cut in numberless different figures, and of small shrubs, either low growing or prevented by shears from running up too high. The whole is fenced in with a wall masked by box trees, which rise in graduated ranks to the top. Beyond the wall lies a meadow which owes as many beauties to nature, as all I have been describing *within* does to art. In one place you have a little meadow; in another the box is interposed in groups, and cut into a thousand different forms; sometimes into letters, expressing the name of the master or again that of the artificer; whilst here and there little obelisks rise intermixed alternately with fruit trees; when on a sudden, in the midst of this elegant regularity, you are surprised with an imitation of the negligent beauties of rural nature; in the centre of which lies a spot surrounded with a knot of dwarf plane trees. Beyond these are interspersed clumps of the smooth and twining acathus; then come a variety of figures and names cut in box.'

This is a wonderful picture of Pliny's garden, but the amount of clipping needed to keep all in perfect shape must have caused weeks of careful work, so I am not surprised by his underlying love of the natural scene. Was it less work or simply just as beautiful? Was this an early moment when the informal garden was competing with the formal? Once again we return to the basic question of why we make gardens. I believe it originates in our desire to create an atmosphere which contrasts with our natural surroundings.

Garden scenes depicted on the walls of the small but formal gardens in Pompeii and Herculaneum helped to establish for the owners an illusion that their patch extended away into the countryside. There were low, painted fences in the foreground enclosing shrubs, trees, statues and fountains; behind were natural views of the open countryside. The actual garden was always formal, and it is evident that formality won, establishing a setting for topiary. And the statues of the artist who used the shears became equal with that of the sculptor who worked in stone.

It requires but little imagination to appreciate how well shapes of topiary stood out against the blue Mediterranean sky, and for me the effect and contrasts of light and shade in Italian gardens are an aesthetic pleasure I always feel inspired to copy when I get home. It is very likely that the Romans brought their art of topiary to Britain nearly 2,000 years ago. Box was their favourite shrub for clipping, and evidence that they used it has been discovered at the Roman sites, although any careful shapes they created did of course disappear in later centuries.

At the Villa Garzoni, Collodi, Italy, the different greens of the ancient, curiously-shaped hedge stand out in silhouette against the bright Italian sky.

A garden at the Château Langeais in the Loire valley, France. This is almost a replica of a French medieval garden with trellis-work ornamented with fleur-de-lys, brick-sided turf benches and simple topiary reflecting the shape of the château's turrets. Unfortunately, the effect is marred by the modern centre-piece and blue crazy-paving.

EUROPEAN TOPIARY

In Cordoba, the centre of Moorish learning in Spain, the Courtyard of the Orange Trees was laid out in the grounds of the celebrated mosque in the year AD 976. The connecting links between mosque and garden were avenues of towering palms and orange trees pruned for better fruiting. Clipped myrtle hedge and regular orange trees placed around a pool constituted the famous Court of the Myrtles in the thirteenth-century Alhambra in Granada. This was not topiary as Pliny described it, but rather the use of controlled shapes with which to build up the pattern of a formal garden.

Illustrations of medieval gardens in Europe show box, cypress and rosemary cut into balls and tiers which frequently became the centrepiece of a small and sparsely planted raised bed. Box edging was sometimes substituted for the trellis work fences used to border the beds. A striking feature of the medieval garden was the arbour. An arbour was made of entwined branches clipped and trained to form a roof over the seat. A practical and attractive form of topiary. King James of Scotland, in prison in Windsor Castle, wrote of the garden he could see from his window:

A garden Faire, and in the corner is set
Ane arbere green, with wandis long and small
Raillit about; and so with treis set
Was all the place and hawthorn hedges knet.

In the sixteenth and seventeenth century, England was becoming increasingly garden conscious, and topiary work gave the imaginative gardener much scope. Leland's *Itinerary* (*c.* 1560) mentions examples of topiary, including the garden at Wresehill Castle, near Howden in Yorkshire. The orchards were outside the moat and in them were 'mounts, *opere topiarii*, writhen about with degrees like the turning of cockle shells to come to the top without payne'. This reminds me of the mount at Packwood, Warwickshire and also of a lesser-known mount made to disguise the ancient dungeon at Beaumesnil near Dieppe. In 1568

'The gardens at Hampton Court were trained, intertwined and trimmed in so wonderful a fashion, and in such extraordinary shapes that the like could not easily be found.'

THE DUKE OF WURZBURG, 1592

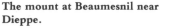

The mount at Beaumesnil near
Dieppe.

Thomas Hill wrote that threads of knots and mazes should be made with hyssop, thyme, lavender cotton and other evergreen herbs which could be kept neatly clipped.

Gervase Markham, in his translation (1616) of *The Country Farm* by Estienne and Leibault, says a low fence round the knot will keep it safe. Lattice work should be about 2 ft (60 cm) high and should then be fashioned into the shapes of battlements, birds and boats with shorter poles or wands, made pliant for the purpose. Now mix whitethorn, eglantine and sweet briar together, and 'as they shoot and grow up, you shall wind and plash them within the Lattice work, ever and anon as need require, either with your sheers or hook, cutting them to that shape and proportion to which you first framed your lattice work.' In fact, a topiary hedge.

William Lawson, the north of England clergyman who died in 1635 after a lifetime of gardening, gives us more first-hand information about gardens than any of his contemporaries. His description of practical gardens for typical manor houses contains little about topiary. But in the 'quarters' nearest the house there should be trees, 'standing in comely order which way soever you look'. Sadly he does not advocate special trees for topiary, but says, 'Your gardener can frame your lesser wood to the shape of men armed in the field, ready to give battel; of swift running greyhounds or of well scented and true running hounds to chase the deer, or hunt the Hare. This kind of hunting shall not waste your corn, nor much your coin.' This indicates that the topiary trees were made into fanciful shapes rather than tiers and balls which might be considered too plain.

We all turn to John Evelyn for sound information about horticulture in the second half of the seventeenth century, a time when topiary was an essential feature of the English garden, both as clipped hedges and tonsored shapes. Evelyn recommends using yew, but comments that 'since the use of bows is laid aside among us, the propagation of the tree is likewise quite forborn; but the neglect of it is to be deplor'd.' I do wish that in the same paragraph he had mentioned the use of yew for topiary. The evergreen he does recom-

'Little low hedges, round like welts, with some pyramids, I like well; and in some places fair columns, upon frames of carpenters work.'

FRANCIS BACON

Phillyrea angustifolia used in the centre of the knot garden at Barnsley House.

mend is *Phillyrea angustifolia* and he wonders why it is planted in cases and treated in the same manner as oranges and lemons, as it is so hardy. 'By long experience I have found it equal our holly in suffering the extremest rigours of our cruellest frosts and winds.' There must be some good reason why phillyrea is neglected, as it happens today as well. Visitors to our garden admire and covet it, but it is not readily available at garden centres. In my opinion standard *Phillyrea angustifolia* would be in every way as attractive and hardy as the standard portugal laurels that are now coming back into fashion. This *phillyrea* also makes beautiful dome-shaped bushes and could be used to great advantage to emphasize corners or as regular squat sentinels to edge a wide path or driveway. I use it as a centrepiece in our knot garden based on a 1583 design, as it is a suitable substitute for box and was cultivated in England in the sixteenth century. Phillyrea has no common name; if it had one would it be more popular, I wonder?

The Anti-Topiary Reaction

The amazing topiary garden at Levens Hall in Cumbria has survived for nearly three centuries in a perfect state. This wonderful achievement was the work of Monsieur Beaumont, a pupil of the famous Le Nôtre, whose portrait hangs in the hall. He also laid out the gardens at Hampton Court, which together with Levens was probably the first place 'in this country in which the genuine art [of topiary] was practised', according to W. Gibson the head gardener at Levens early in the present century.

Levens is so striking that visitors could well feel that a topiary garden is beyond their scope and the span of their years. Time, however, had nothing to do with the decline in the popularity of topiary early in the eighteenth century. Its excessive use was the culprit. Two writers, Addison in the *Spectator* and Pope in the *Guardian*, began the crusade against topiary.

The topiary garden at Levens Hall in Cumbria, laid out between 1701 and 1703 for Colonel James Graham at that time treasurer to James II.

Not only were many tonsored shapes cut down, but carefully trimmed hedges were allowed to sprout in all directions, and avenues of trees were destroyed—all in the name of 'improvement'. Change is essential to stimulate progress and we are fortunate that grand gardens such as those at Levens and Melbourne, Powis Castle and Chastleton House have survived the centuries. But the dictates of fashion pass the lesser gardens by, and where a cottage owner has no wish to follow the current trend we can often see lovely examples of peacocks guarding the entrance to the garden.

From about 1860 it became not unusual for a few specimen topiary bushes to be added to the formal bedded-out garden, perhaps to tone down the glaring geraniums and calceolarias. The great yew hedges at Sudeley Castle date from the 1840s. Leopold de Rothschild made a topiary sundial at Ascott, Wing; suits of playing cards were planted in a new knot garden at Ludstone Hall in Shropshire; and the famous Sermon on the Mount at Packwood in Warwickshire dates from the middle of the century. As you will notice, these are all in large gardens and, it was considered, fitted into the scale.

Left: **Impeccable cottage topiary in satisfying symmetrical shapes.**

Right: **The Sermon on the Mount at Packwood, Warwickshire.**

'A stone hewn into a gracefully ornamental vase or urn, has value which it did not possess, a yew hedge clipped, is only defaced. The one is a production of art, the other a distortion of nature.'

SIR WALTER SCOTT

Topiary Revived

At the turn of the century there were two established firms of nurserymen exhibiting at shows and supplying examples of topiary, William Cutbush and Son of Highgate, London, and Messrs. Cheal and Son of Crawley Surrey. Mr. Cutbush travelled frequently to Holland where the art of topiary never died out. He persuaded Dutch nurserymen to sell him some of their best specimens, and when this source of supply began to run out he travelled the countryside and found movable bushes in farm and cottage gardens. And so demand in England was satisfied whilst the English nurserymen built up a supply of oncoming bushes.

Box and yew are the trees most often used to create shapes of sitting hens, ducks and geese, with dogs to protect them, or spirals, columns and pyramids surmounted with balls or peacocks, or just simple mop-heads. Compared with the list in Pope's anti-topiary tirade, the shapes are most modest, even practical. These choice figures were planted around the country but in most cases, during the war years, were left to grow at random and so lost their choice shapes and thus their meaning. Now once again I sense a trend back to using clipped shapes as striking features in our gardens.

Three prestigious gardens in England, Sissinghurst, Great Dixter and Hidcote, all have topiary in varying degrees, as do many others. The topiary garden at Great Dixter, made by Christopher Lloyd's father Nathaniel, has felt established and beautiful for more than sixty years. The solidity and permanence of the forms give great pleasure.

Now is the moment to think about the revival rather than the survival of topiary, and the extent to which, from a practical point of view, it can be used in present-day gardens. Supply often lags behind demand, especially when a finished product takes years to achieve. Topiary is a slow process and the gardener must decide whether he has enough patience (or years to live) to plant small bushes which he can train on himself or if he will look for and plant larger specimens. These last are not readily available and the risk in moving them is considerably greater than with smaller bushes. Then there is always the hope that an existing shrub in the garden can be transformed into an attractive shape. Old holly bushes can quite easily be trimmed into tiers or pyramids. Old box trees and yew will both shoot from a branch or trunk, and by hard clipping an untidy box bush can be made to look like a respectable cube or pyramid as long as one is bold with the shears. Remember that flexible branches may be tied into the shape you want. Imagination is the key word. There is a final key to effective topiary: you must enjoy the visual and actual pleasure of doing it.

Practical Topiary

'It may be true, as I believe it is, that the natural form of a tree is the most beautiful possible, but it may happen that we do not always want the most beautiful form, but one of our own designing, and expressive of our ingenuity.'

SHIRLEY HIBBERD

The first necessity is to choose a tree or shrub which will tolerate being clipped not just occasionally but every year, twice a year. One with small leaves is, for obvious reasons, much more appropriate than large-leafed evergreens such as the Victorian laurel (*Aucuba*). It is pointless starting on a shrub which is doubtfully hardy unless you can protect it in times of exceptionally hard frost or have it in a tub that can be brought inside.

YEW (*Taxus baccata*)

The most often used tree for topiary and for well clipped hedges and archways nowadays is yew. One is always given the impression that yew grows slowly and take years to become a well-established hedge. This is not so. If the ground is well prepared, and the after-care is good, yew grows several inches a year. My experience is that a 2 ft (60 cm) yew hedge will be 5 ft (150 cm) after five years; an averge growth rate of 8 in (20 cm) a year, allowing for only 4 in (10 cm) in the first year after planting. After fifteen years the hedge could look as though it had been there for a generation. Yew is a long-lived tree and may be pruned severely. If your hedge becomes too broad, which it could well do, making clipping difficult along the top, you can cut one side right back to the main stem. Do this in early spring and by the next August new green growth will have appeared all up the trunk; after two years there will be enough growth to let you start clipping again in earnest. Often only one side of a hedge is seen frequently, the other being less in view; if this is so, cut back the latter.

Before planting prepare the ground well, digging a wide trench and adding well-rotted manure sufficiently deep so that the roots of your new bushes will not come in contact with it. Spring is the best time to plant, especially where the site is exposed. It is important to remember that wind can rock the roots of newly planted shrubs and so cause unseen damage. Ways of preventing this are by staking or protecting with a line of rigid netting, especially marketed for the purpose. Newly planted evergreens must be watered

Topiary at Great Dixter, East
Sussex.

The circular tank at Hidcote,
Gloucestershire surrounded by
carefully clipped yew walls.

in the summer during rainless weeks. I follow the philosophy of the great tree-man. Richard Sr. Barb. Baker,' and place a flat stone beside the stem of a newly planted tree to conserve moisture. In fact we always surround the stems and even during the driest periods if you pick one up you will find the soil has not dried out under the stone. Allow your yews to settle for at least a year before you start clipping; this will give the roots time to get growing. If you cut the leading shoot this will cause the lower ones to fill out. The best time to clip yew is in late August and early September in England, and with a hedge, by the second clipping you should make sure you have an even and compact effect.

Planting distance for a hedge varies with the height of the yews. If possible 2½ – 3 ft (75 – 90 cm) is best unless the plants are very small, in which case they should be put closer. It is vitally important to remember an annual feed; a general purpose fertilizer in March is ideal.

A hedge should have a feeling of permanence and substance, and the surest way to produce this effect is to give it a sloping face or 'batter'. Visit the garden at Great Dixter and you will understand immediately. The hedges here were planted with tremendous precision and the result is still wonderful after more than sixty years. According to the late Nathaniel Lloyd's estimate, a yew hedge should have from 2 – 4 in (5 – 10 cm) batter for each 1 ft (30 cm) of height. This will allow the lower branches to receive adequate sun and air, essential if they are to remain well clothed right down to the ground. To maintain this accurately, you must have a simple measuring device. It is equally important to keep the height of the hedge quite level, and again a simple wooden structure such as a pole with a cross bar can be adapted.

With the help of modern equipment clipping should be a pleasure, but it does require practice. In days gone by, the head gardener in his trilby hat must have trained his underlings to help when the moment came for autumn clipping. Today the head gardener is probably the owner and he or she must learn the hard way, by trial and error. Perhaps it would be as well to take the advice of the head gardener at Levens eighty years ago. 'When it is found necessary to employ a person to do any part of the clipping who has not had any previous experience, he should only be allowed to begin on trees of the least importance…The beginner will always find that a round or oval shaped tree is a great deal less difficult to work upon than a square one or a hedge.'

Understandable.

BOX (*Buxus sempervirens*)

This is a fascinating plant to work with. It seems almost indestructible, will stand severe clipping and cutting back and is one of the few shrubs you can plant deeply in the soil. Bury a long portion of its woody stem as well as the roots and after a year it will have formed a mass of new fibrous roots all along the stem. You can make new plants from old very easily this way. Conventional cuttings taken in autumn and spring (preferably the latter) will root within a year. If you are planning a box edging it saves time to put the cuttings directly into their final position. Put them close together, say 3 in (8 cm) apart, and your new edging will soon be beautifully firm.

In Britain the varieties most frequently seen are *Buxus sempervirens* and *B.s.* 'Suffruticosa'. Eventually, if left unpruned, the common *B.sempervirens* will make a small tree. This variety has many cultivars with different-shaped leaves. Their Latin names will explain their characteristics: *pendula* (pendulous), *prostrata* (prostrate), *rotundifolia* (round-leaved), *argentea* (silver). Suffruticosa is the cultivar that has been used for centuries for edging. It grows slowly, has a small obovate leaf and may be kept quite low by constant clipping. If it is left unclipped and untended for years, however, it will probably become leafless at the base. There are two ways of treating this. Mound up soil around the bare stems and forget about it for a year or more whilst it makes new roots along the stems. Then dig the whole thing up and make a fresh

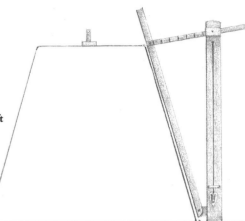

Left: To plant a yew hedge, place individual trees 18 in (45cm) apart in a trench. Fill bottom of trench with manure, and ensure that roots are planted above it. Stake trees and place flat stones beside the stems to conserve moisture.

Right: Instrument for measuring the 'batter' of a yew hedge. The cross-piece at the top is marked with lines, each of which represents 1 in (3 cm) batter to 1 ft (30 cm) in height. A peg passing through a hole in the upright to holes in the cross-piece keeps the angle the same. On top of the hedge is a spirit-level on a plank for checking that the top is kept flat.

start, removing the old roots and using the newly rooted pieces. Alternatively, dig it all up at once, make a deep trench and lay the box (roots and all) diagonally along the trench and leave it for a year or more. You will then discover that marvellous new roots have grown along the stem. Cut off the old roots and you will have a good supply of box edging for your new knot garden or for outlining your beds.

The Balearic box will grow into a small tree and is quite suitable for making into large shapes. The leaves are larger, rounder and thicker, but I doubt that it is as hardy as the common box. Probably the most hardy variety is *Buxus microphylla Koreana*, which is grown in the north eastern states of the USA for its hardiness.

We are always told that box harbours slugs. Probably this is true, but we often read that 'the weather lately has favoured slugs', so the best thing to do is to take precautions anyway. That box has greedy roots is certainly another truism. The way to deal with this in box edging is simply to dig straight down with a spade, quite close to the box, and so sever the wandering roots. The smell of box puts some people off and apparently Queen Anne had all the box removed from Hampton Court garden because she disliked its odour. In my experience most people like it, especially when it is in flower.

Old box bushes will survive being moved relatively well, but they are becoming more and more difficult to find. If you do have one in your garden which has an interesting shape, stand back and observe it, and decide how you can improve it quite simply by clipping. Box does not lend itself to specially artistic efforts. Easy shapes such as buns or squares, sitting ducks or plain pyramids are best. Leave the peacocks to the yew.

When you are creating something new from box, remember that if you cannot find a large bush, several smaller ones planted close together, and where necessary tied together, will give an instant effect. Always use tarred string for this or the corslet effect may suddenly snap.

BAY (*Laurus nobilis*)

This evergreen aromatic shrub is an ancient plant. The Romans made wreaths of 'laurus' or bay to crown their victorious soldiers. John Gerrard in his herbal of 1597 says, 'The bay tree grows naturally in Spain, we plant, and set it in gardens, defending it from cold, in March especially.' Frost may cut it to the ground, but it usually grows again from the roots. This happened to our bay in spring 1982 and in two summers it has recovered vigorously to a height of at least 3 ft (90 cm). Today it is more usual in England to see bay planted in tubs and clipped into pyramids or standard balls. The trees are very attractive like this and the clippings may be kept for cooking. Take cuttings in July.

HAWTHORN (*Crataegus*)

Hawthorn trees can be clipped into attractive balls or cubes on standard stems, and a line of these is a good way of outlining the boundary of a vegetable garden or a cottage garden. An avenue kept neatly trimmed makes an unpretentious feature for a farm driveway. Clip them in early August after next year's flower buds have formed and growth has stopped for that season. Buy well-shaped standard or half-standards.

ROSEMARY

Rosemary is neither as long-lived nor as hardy a box or yew, so treat it with respect. Growing it against a wall, as they did in Elizabethan times, is an excellent idea. In the sixteenth century, the walls at Hampton Court were covered with clipped rosemary. In our garden the only rosemary bush which was not killed during the cold winter of 1982/83 was growing against a south-east-facing wall. All the other rosemaries died, including a six-year-old clipped hedge which had formed a firm barrier about 2 ft (60 cm) high and as much through. Clipping rosemary results in most but not all of the flowers being lost, as it blooms on the new wood. Rosemary cuttings root very easily, even from hard wood.

Colours and textures in hedges. *Left: Tropaeolum speciosum* growing through yew. This is difficult to establish, but once achieved will improve year by year. *Centre*: Tapestry hedge showing yew, copper beech and holly. *Right*: Variegated and green holly and yew in the same hedge.

HOLLY (*Ilex*)

As John Evelyn discovered, the common holly, *Ilex aquifolium*, makes a wonderful hedge, and our hollies, clipped and unclipped, give us great pleasure all through the year, especially in winter. Holly is very accommodating to clipping. Use secateurs rather than shears, so as to achieve an accurate cut just above a node. There are many varieties of holly to choose from. So many, that is, until it comes to the moment of purchase and then it is difficult to find what you have set your heart on. My advice is to buy and plant whatever is available and treat it as your nurseryman recommends.

My choice for clipping is *Ilex x altaclarensis* 'Golden King', which has a bold leaf margined with gold. Despite its name it is female and will give you berries even when you clip. *I.a.* 'Silver Queen' is male, make no mistake, and will provide a pollinator for your females. Put one amongst your females and you should have berries for Christmas. Immediately you become aware of the joys of topiary you will also realize its limitations and also its virtues and possibilities. Small leaves will create an intricate design, and the larger the leaf the less detail is possible. Holly produces lovely bold effects—hedges, balls and tiers, even spirals. But these are things you must create yourself, or direct with exactness, otherwise the final result may not be worthwhile. The quality of holly lies in its ability to grow directly from the bud to which you have clipped it, for there is little 'die back'.

LONICERA

Lonicera nitida and *L.n.* 'Baggesen's Gold' grow very vigorously and have small dense leaves. As a hedge they grow almost too fast and require clipping twice a year, but for quick-effect topiary they are ideal. Their small leaves favour a neat clip and they are extremely hardy. The golden variety needs full sun to keep its colour and also protection from the worst winds. While you are waiting for your box balls to grow why not try a few lonicera ones?

'Any ladies that please may have their own effigies in Myrtle, or their husband's in Hornbeam.'

ALEXANDER POPE, 1713

PRIVET (*Ligustrum*)

Privet makes a useful hedge. I prefer the golden variety, *L. ovalifolium aureum*, when grown as specimen bushes rather than as a hedge. It clips well into balls or pyramids and can be an outstanding feature in a mixed border or at a focal point, in the same way as the golden lonicera. I use both of these shrubs in our garden and it is surprising how frequently people comment on them favourably.

OLD ENGLISH LAVENDER (*Lavendula*)

Lavender hedges and edges are usual, but in the summer of 1983 the National Trust grew lavender as standards on 18-in (48-cm) stems and it looked sensational.

HORNBEAM (*Carpinus betulus*)

The common hornbeam clips well. One unusual way I saw it grown in France was against a wall supporting a terrace. Hornbeams were planted in groups of four at intervals of 9 ft (2.75 m) and then clipped to form archways against the wall in which pots of geraniums were placed. This is a theme which could be used with different plants and on varying scales. A wall 1O ft (3 m) high or more could have a hedge-like covering of hornbeam with archways, with espaliered fruit trees, such as peaches or plums inserted into them, and a *trompe l'oeil* trellis to simulate a series of *allees* through the wall. The ideas are endless—I might decide on a seat in each niche for contemplation.

Phillyrea angustifolia

I have mentioned this shrub and sung its praises earlier. I can only hope it will become more readily available at nurseries than it is now. Treat it in exactly the same manner as box.

Hornbeam arches add interest under the balustraded terrace at the Château de Limpeville.

CHAPTER NINE

WATER IN THE GARDEN

Any garden ornament or piece of architecture mirrored in water receives an addition to its dignity by the repetition and continuation of upright line.

GERTRUDE JEKYLL 1901

'Water is the life and soul of a garden, whether on the ground plot of a suburban cottage, or the embellished lawn of an extensive villa'. This was Shirley Hibberd's opinion as he expressed it in the third edition of *Rustic Adornments of Homes of Taste* in 1870. The first edition (1856) had no mention of water in the garden. Was this a reflection of the evolution of taste in nineteenth-century England?

Today we regard the use of water, natural or artificial, moving or still as an essential, or, at least, an important feature in our gardens. Special liners for pools and electric pumps for fountains have brought ponds and water jets within the scope of any gardener with a hankering for water.

Quiet water creates reflections, calms our spirits, provides a special place in which to grow water lilies and other aquatic plants and a home for the silently gliding goldfish. Children and grown-ups watch enthralled as the fish come to feed. Turn on the fountain and the scene immediately changes, the pictures in the reflections are shattered, the fish become animated, and the movement and sound of the rising and falling of the water breaks the silence, bringing a feeling of companionship.

The corners of this formal pool at Filoli near San Francisco are marked with clipped bushes of *Teucrium frutescens*. The use of a single theme for the water planting, such as these bullrushes, is appropriate for a formal pool.

Having once decided to include water in your garden, you must first choose the site and the type of pool which will best harmonize with your garden design. If you have a formal parterre or rose garden then a round or symmetrically shaped pond in the centre with a raised cut-stone edging, and with a simple fountain will fit in. This presents no problems aside from those of getting the shape and the price right. The formality will demand no planting round the pool and a minimum of very simple planting in the water; probably a single theme, such as water lilies or *Apogoneton distachyus,* the water hawthorn so named for its strong scent of may blossom, and a single group of arum lilies, *Zantedeschia aethiopica,* or another plant with a taller and spikier leaf than the water lilies.

In another situation you might decide that you have the right spot for a symmetrical pool with a formal edging of stones at ground level, the water either flush with the stones or an inch or two lower. The former is often good in a confined space, or where the water may easily be topped up. If your water level is lower than the edging, the stones should always overhang the water. This is important, for it prevents the sometimes unattractive line between water and edging, especially where the water is inclined to evaporate in the summer. Again, no plants are needed round the pool and you may choose between plants and reflections in the water. Elegant plants in elegant pots may be stood around the pool to enhance its shape and add more reflections.

If you have a sunken garden, shady round its perimeter, with ferns, foliage, plants, hellebores, groups of lilies, and cool plants, then make a pool in the centre or at one end in proportion to the size and shape of the area. This is the classic place for a pool without edging, one where the lawn merges with the water and after rain (always an exciting moment in the garden) the water will overflow into the grass. It will be a predominantly green garden with reflections in the water of clouds and blue sky. Remember that the brightness of the water will stand out in clear contrast to its surroundings and the greater the area of sky that is reflected the larger your pool will appear, so my choice would be for no plants in the water, and none on the edges either. They would destroy the purpose of the pool's melting into the surrounding grass and make an unwanted division between lawn and reflections.

Another pool requiring no plants in the ground around it is one that has raised sides

Firm outlines by a pool will ensure interesting reflections, although it is essential to keep the water clear.

The water hawthorn, *Apogoneton distachyus,* is one of the easiest of water plants to grow and should be allowed to occupy a pool on its own.

built of brick or stone chosen according to the natural building material of your district. To be practical, the sides should be just the right height for sitting on. In this case I would make the pond deep with a dark mysterious bottom so that, as you look into it, you can see your own reflection or that of your companion. You could stand pots of plants on the wall and these would be reflected too. Make the depth of the water such that you can just touch it with your hands as you lean in—perhaps even a bit higher. Your fountain here will of necessity be an upright jet so that you will not be sprayed as you sit. A single water lily is all that is required and, if you could get them established, a few ferns growing in the inside of the north-facing part of the wall just above the water's surface. I imagine this pool to be round or oval. In order to produce this dark look in the water, it must be small. This type of pool is best built with cement sides and treated to make it water-proof up as high as the water level. Above the water level the bricks or stone will be visi-ble. A raised pond will take on the character of a tank when the water is flush with the top of the sides and can spill over, growing green, mossy effects. (The best methods for creating pools is discussed at the end of the chapter.)

You may decide that you want a pond for the express purpose of creating a home for moisture-loving plants. This is what happened in our garden. We wanted primulas and other moisture plants but an informal pool would have looked uncomfortable in the setting. Instead we chose the place where we most often sit, made a rectangular pond and surrounded it on three sides with narrow beds which were part of the water-retentive area.

A terrace pool reflecting the bright Canadian sky in the garden owned by Anne and Frank Cabot. To achieve the maximum reflections water should lap the rim of the pool.

A bank of shrubs surrounds the water at Crittenden.

A beautifully moulded stone surround to the small circular pool at La Mortola, near Mentone, in Italy.

At Barnsley House narrow beds were created each side of the pond to form a home for moisture-loving plants.

'It behoveth to have a well in the garden, unless some running water, as either ditch or small river be near adjoining, for that sweet water sprinkled on young plants and herbes, giveth a special nourishment. If a well be lacking then dig a deep pit in some convenient place in the garden'.

THOMAS HILL, 1577.

This was in the days before the invention of pond liners. All the surfaces then had to be cemented and made waterproof. Holes were drilled at quite a high level between the pool and the beds to allow just enough water through to keep the beds moist. The main plants in these were marsh marigolds, mimulus, *Iris siberica* and *Primula florindae*.

Informal pools give you much more scope for using moisture-loving plants. You must, of course, choose your site carefully. If your garden is flat then try to keep away from a formally planted area, and place your pool further away from the house where such a pool might naturally occur. If your garden site has different levels then do not choose the highest point. It will seem out of keeping there. Streams on a hillside start as a trickle and form pools lower down the hill when they have gathered more water. A still pool in too much shade will soon go stagnant or become covered with weeds, so pick a sunny place which will not become a trap for fallen leaves in the autumn. The depth will depend on the variety of water lilies you want, or, of course, you could decide on the depth required and then select the lilies; they require anything from 10 – 30 in (25 cm – 75 cm) of water. The strong growers spread too profusely for small pools, so my advice is to send for a reliable catalogue, or even two, which will give you specialized information. Different depths can be established when you are building your pool by making shelves and having a shallow and a deep end.

The right conditions for marginal plants can be made in several ways. When you are using a flexible Butyl liner buy enough to bury the edge for two or three feet, at least 6 in (15 cm) below the level of the surrounding ground, finally bringing it up where you want your marginal planting to end. Soil alone on top of this would mostly wash straight into the pool so mix it with pebbles and larger stones into which you can put your plants,

Constructing a simple pool.
1. Lay out a rope or hose to the required shape and size and start digging round the inside to outline the basic shape.

2. Cut the sides with an inward slope of 3 in (7 cm) across for every 9 in (23 cm) down, incorporating a marginal shelf if required. Place a plank across the pool to support a spirit-level to check that the top of the pool is level. Repeat for the marginal shelf.

3. Having removed sharp stones, lay Butyl or similar liner loosely in the pool. Weigh down edges with bricks or other heavy objects and start to fill with water. As the pool fills, lift off weights at intervals to allow the liner to fit neatly.

4. When the pool is full, trim excess liner leaving at least 4 in (10 cm) overlap. Finally, lay paving round pool on top of liner, or make turf sides as described in the text.

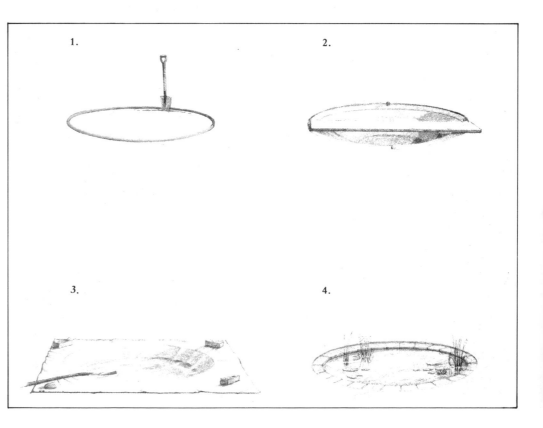

those which like a moist root run but not totally submerged roots. There is a list at the end of this chapter of plants for different situations.

Another idea is to overlap the surrounding turf down into the water. When the hole for the pool is being excavated at least 2 ft (60 cm) of turf should be folded back on to the sides. When the pool lining has been made, the turf can be pushed back into the water. It will hide the edge, be it concrete or Butyl, and give the surrounding soil a good moist texture for marginal plants. This creates as natural a look as possible and keeps the soil damp in the hottest weather so long as your pool remains well filled. This kind of pool is the right setting for bold foliage, hardy flowers such as many of the irises and *Lobelia cardinalis*, striking plants which need more moisture than the herbaceous border will provide.

You may be fortunate enough to have a natural lake or pond in your garden. If you have, the marginal planting will be the same as for an informal pond, but remember it is sometimes pleasant to be able to see the water's edge.

So far we have only thought about still water but the electric pump has transformed the availability of fountains. Go to a good firm and you will find jets to suit your taste, ranging from a single spray to multi-jets capable of making as grand a display as anything at Versailles. Fountains have many fascinations—their own pattern, the spray, the design of the splashing on the water surface and its sound. The movement of water creates negative ions which are known to give us a feeling of well-being. We have a fountain which sprays its water on to a vertical stone surface and so creates an extra sound of water on stone.

The great chain of fountains at Longwood Gardens when lit up at night are like an amazing display of fireworks. The jets which play on Fifth Avenue, New York in front of the Metropolitan Museum have a definite and compelling effect of slowing one down.

Left: Illuminated fountains at Versailles.

Right: A hidden water garden at the Generaliffe, Granada, in Spain, where regularly spaced single water jets make a soothing pattern.

Those along the watercourse at the Generaliffe Gardens in Granada catch the strong sunshine and give a feeling of coolness. At the Villa d'Este in Italy it is again quite different: you feel wonderment that anything could have been so grandly contrived so long ago, as you move from one episode to the next.

It is no longer probable that we could afford to build great cascades as at Chatsworth or twin 'Butterfly' lakes like those at Middleton Place in South Carolina or magnificent water parterres as in many old French gardens, but we can go and enjoy them and wonder at the technical skills of the men who with a minimum of mechanical aids were able to devise such elaborate waterworks.

Those gardeners who are lucky enough to have natural moving water are most fortunate. Any such garden can never be dull, for there is always variety and, aside from plants, water attracts its own brand of wildlife. One of my favourite gardens in which water plays a major role is an old vicarage in Gloucestershire with the River Windrush as one boundary. The owners have made the very best of it. From the river they have cut a network of narrow channels to create islands and different contours on a small area of land not more than 45 ft (13.75 m) each way. This has made a wonderful home for hundreds of primulas, whose colour and interest last from March until October, the climax coming in June. There are willows of forty different varieties, providing catkins in spring, coloured bark in winter and changing greens in summer. These in turn give shade to the plants on the banks of the channels, and here there are campanulas, hardy geraniums, saxifrage and ground-covering vincas. They call this the wild garden and have separated it from the formal, Lutyens- style garden with a high wall. This formal part is of the same width as the Georgian house.

The wonder of water, some falling some rising, at the Villa d'Este garden, in Italy.

Above: The grand cascade at Chatsworth where the waterworks were all contrived by Sir Joseph Paxton in the mid-nineteenth century.

Above left: A more practical inspiration for today's gardener is to be found at Villarceau in France.

Left: A part of the willow and primula garden at the Old Rectory, Naunton, Gloucestershire, the home of the Rt. Hon. Nicholas and Mrs. Ridley, referred to in the text.

They planted a copper beech hedge on the one side to complement the wall opposite. Nearest the house is a circular pool with stone surround and from this a narrow canal stretches under a classical bridge towards a summer house recently built in the owner's own time at precious weekends. Brick columns stride along one side and carry an aqueduct used as a clever device for a watering system in summer. In his obsession for water the owner has made yet a third water garden. This time it is a sunken garden with soil damp enough to grow moisture loving plants. To give it special character it has signs of the zodiac carved along the inner rim of the low retaining walls. So in this garden of only one acre we have three distinct kinds of water garden: a wild stream garden, a formal setting and a boggy area enclosed by a low retaining wall. The charm of this garden lies in the exuberance of planting which complements the architectural features and thrives on the moisture-laden soil. Another of its attractions for me is the knowledge that everything I see there, except the fortuitous presence of the river and the old trees, has been created slowly over the years by one dedicated craftsman who looks upon it as a hobby and has done everything himself.

FALLING WATER

'One of the greatest ornaments to a garden is a fountain, but many fountains are curiously ineffective. A fountain is most beautiful when it leaps into the air, and you can see it against a background of green foliage.'

HENRY BRIGHT 1881.

Part of the experience of being by moving water is its sound. Sitting beside a pool in the evening, you will want a fountain gentle enough to create just enough sound and movement to give you a feeling of companionship but not so much as to cause a distraction. The pattern of ever widening ripples will hold your attention. The higher and more elaborate your water jets, the greater will be the noise of the falling water, but like all other features the fountain jet should relate in scale to its surroundings. The fountains at Versailles are magnificent in their setting, but would be ludicrously out of place in an enclosed space.

Our own fountain is at the end of a vista. We wished to hear the water from a distance but knew that a high jet would be quite out of keeping with the informality of its site. Simon Verity who was carving the stonework for us had the inspiration of making the water play on to a flat stone through the mouths of four fat frogs. This has two sounds, first the water hitting the stone and then another note as it drops into the pool beneath. Water lends itself to the use of sculpture and you should attempt to be original and discover artists who can create something beautiful, reflecting your own feeling in the garden. Simon made our fountain in 1972 and his great talent has been acknowledged by Sir Roy Strong at whose commission he has carved beautiful lettering at the entrance to the Henry Cole Wing at the Victoria and Albert Museum.

There are two surprising water features in the heart of New York city. Greenacre Park, consisting of three lots on East 51st Street between 2nd and 3rd Avenue, has a dramatic waterfall on the back wall cascading over giant granite blocks. These blocks are recessed into the wall so give the feeling of a natural waterfall down which the amazing quantity of 5,000 gallons tumble every minute and are then recirculated. It is quite an experience sitting in this small 'park', surrounded by plants and the sound of rushing water which together successfully subdue not only the drone of traffic but also the awareness of being in the centre of incessant activity. I was first told about this wonderful place to sit and unwind from a feeling of bustle by Barry Ferguson, a New Zealander, and an artist in planting and flower arrangement, who has been in charge of the plantings since 1972. He is justifiably proud that this 'Vest Pocket' park has become the outdoor room for many New Yorker's and is kept in constantly immaculate trim.

On a still summer day, nothing is more delightful than to sit quite still and listen to the sounds of the water of the little rills. Their many voices may almost be likened to a form of speech.

GERTRUDE JEKYLL 1901

Another small sanctuary is on 53rd Street between Fifth and Madison. Paley Park was constructed in 1967 and since then thousands of people have been able to relax there every day. It is raised above the street level and a 20-foot wall of falling water occupies the entire background. It is cool, refreshing and hypnotic. There are chairs and tables for comfort and a grove of honey locust trees to give shade. Walking into it from the noisy street and the roar of the traffic instantly changes your mood; I believe this is largely due to the motion of the water.

Left: Candelabra primulas growing in boggy soil in the zodiac garden at the Old Rectory, Naunton.

Right: Fountain at the Villa Noailles, so covered with moss and lichen that even the stone gives the impression of soaking up the water.

Simon Verity's fountain at Barnsley House with frogs spouting water at a flat surface of spangled Purbeck stone. The surrounding planting was designed mostly for foliage effect.

Nymphaea x marliacea albida.

Plants to use with Water

I have kept to plants which are usually available in specialist nurseries and good garden centres.

WATER LILIES *Nymphaea*

Plants that are distinct of habit and large of leaf always look well near water.

GERTRUDE JEKYLL 1901

Water lilies like sunshine. Most are easy to grow but all require careful planting. Unlike herbaceous plants and trees they must be planted while they are in active growth, from April until August. They make considerable root growth with the result they succeed best if planted direct into soil at the bottom of your pool. When your pool is empty, cover the bottom with 6 – 8 in (15 – 20 cm) of soil and tread this well down. Plant your lilies direct into this and lay stones or old bricks on the roots to keep them anchored. If you must use containers make sure that they are large enough, 12 in (30 cm) square and 4 in (10 cm) deep at the very least. Spread the roots out well having the growing point just above soil level. If planting direct into an empty pool you can make an enclosure with brick or stones, fill it with heavy soil, then plant into this and add a few stones on top. If your pool is already full and you do not wish to empty it, plant your lilies in loose-weave baskets and let these down gently into the water. Always fill your pool slowly in order to minimize the soil disturbance.

Water lilies are perennials, and the leaves die down in late autumn. They are among the least demanding of plants, for not even the dying flower heads and leaves need to be taken off; they will quickly sink to the bottom, disintegrate, rot and become plant food.

When you order young plants you should never expect them to arrive before late May. If you are making a new pool you can delay planting until August.

Colours range from white, through pink, red and yellow. There are no hardy blue water lilies, if you have seen them on your travels these are the tender tropical varieties.

STRONG GROWING VARIETIES FOR WATER UP TO 3 FT (1 M) DEEP
White
N. 'Gladstonia': enormous blooms with yellow centres.
N. 'Gloire de Temple-sur-Lot': incurved petals.

Nymphaea 'Gonnere'.

Pink and Rose
N. amabilis pale salmon pink star-shaped flowers held above the surface.
N. 'masaniello': easily established, large paeony shaped blooms.
N. 'Mrs. Richmond': pale rose, very vigorous and free flowering.

Crimson and Red
N. 'Escarboucle': abundant, perfectly shaped, 'the brightest jewel in the water garden.'

Yellow
N. 'Colonel A.J. Welch': narrow petalled flowers of canary yellow.

MEDIUM GROWERS FOR WATER UP TO 2 FT (60 CM) DEEP.
White
N. marliacea albida: very reliable.
N. 'Gonnere': pure white, very double.

Pink and Rose
N. marliacea 'Rosea': outstanding.
N. marliacea 'Carnea': free blooming.
N. 'René Gerard': rich rose pink.

Crimson and Red
N. 'Gloriosa': should be a first choice.
N. 'James Brydon': Carmen Pink, purple-shaded leaves. Good choice for a shady pool.
N. 'Sultan': cherry-red streaked with white.
N. 'William Falconer': very deep shade of blood red with yellow anthers.

Yellow
N. marliacea 'Chromatella': primrose yellow.

N. 'Moorei': pale sulphur yellow, mabrled green and brown leaves.
N. 'Graziella': orange-yellow.

MODERATELY VIGOROUS FOR WATER UP TO 30 IN (45 CM)
White
N. 'Albatross': the best white for small pools.

Pink and Rose shades
N. 'Joanne Pring': also suitable for tubs.
N. odorata 'Luciana Rose': pink with flowers held above the surface; scented.
N. odorata 'Turicensis': soft rose; scented.
N. odorata 'William Shaw': shell pink, star shaped; scented.
N. 'Rose Arey': cerise pink with orange stamens.

Crimson and Red
N. 'Froebeli': blood-red excellent for small pools.
N. 'Maurice Laydeker': deep rose red with white markings.

Yellow
N. 'Sunrise': large deep yellow, abundantly flowering once the plant is established.

VARIETIES SUITABLE FOR TUBS AND SHALLOW WATER UP TO 1 FT (30 CM) DEEP
White
N. candida: small white starry flowers and correspondingly small leaves.
N. pygmea alba: a perfect miniature; can also be grown in bowls indoors.

Pink and Rose Shades
N. 'Laydekeri Lilacea': rose-lilac spotted with carmine. Ideal for tubs and shallow pools.
N. 'Laydekeri Purpurata': wine red; outer petal lilac pink.

Yellow
N. pygmaea helvola, pale primrose; excellent for shallow water.
N.B. All the Laydekeri varieties take a season to settle after which they flower profusely.
Water lilies are lovely cut flowers, but as they close in late afternoon a few drops of paraffin wax or candle grease should be dropped at the base of the petals to keep them open.

SURFACE-FLOWERING AQUATIC PLANTS
Aponogeton distachyus: flowers from April until October and is suitable for a shady pool, but does better in sunshine; it requires 18 in (50 cm) of water; the forked flower spikes held just above the surface are white with black anthers and are strongly scented.
Hottonia palustris: the water violet; its decorative pale green leaves stay under water and white or lavender-blue flower spikes stand up a few inches above the surface; acts as oxygentor.
Orontium aquaticum: the golden club; needs at least 18 in (50 cm) of soil and only 10 in (25 cm) of water to produce its yellow poker flowers.
Ranuculus aquatilis: the water crowfoot; will grow in still or moving water, with profuse white flowers. Submerged leaves are feathery while the floating leaves are broader; acts as oxygenator.

Orontium Aquaticum.

FREE-FLOATING AQUATICS REQUIRING NO SOIL
Azolla caroliniana: Fairy Floating Moss; use only in small areas where you can control it.
Eichornia speciosa major: the water hyacinth.
Stratiotes aloides

MARGINAL PLANTS
Acorus calamus:the sweet flag; aromatic foliage 2 – 3 ft (60 – 90 cm).
A. calamus variegatus
Butomus umbellatus: flower rush 2 – 3 ft (60 – 90 cm).
Calla palustris: the bog arum; white flowers are not conspicuous but they are followed by scarlet seeds which are showy.
Calthe palustris: the marsh marigold or kingcup; there is a white form, also double yellow. These are all about 1 ft (30 cm), there is a giant form about 3 ft (1 m) tall.
Glyceria aquatica variegata: very showy with shaped leaves, striped green, white and yellow; 18 in (50 cm).
Iris laevigata
I. pseudacorus: our native yellow iris.
I. pseudacorus variegata
Lobelia cardinalis: yes, you really can grow this in 2 – 3 in (5 – 7 cm) of water although it is usually considered a plant for moist soil.
Mentha aquatica: the water mint has a lovely minty smell and pretty lavender flowers and it helps to keep the water clear.
Mimulus in variety: the musk flower; a long flowering plant.
Myosotis palustris: the water forget-me-not.
Pontederia cordata: spikes of blue flowers and upstanding leaves.
Scirpus in variety: the ornamental rushes.
Typha are referred to as bullrushes, their correct common name is reed mace; you can have them in size from 18 in – 3 ft (45 – 90 cm).
Zantedeschia aethiopica: the white arum, usually grown in a cool house.

Iris pseudocorus, the native yellow
flag iris.

Iris Pseudacorus.

Astilbe make good plants for the water edge.

Waterside Plants

These are plants which like a moist soil but not a waterlogged one. I have not described them as most have been mentioned elsewhere in the book. When you are planting your marginal plants draw out your plan carefully so that you have contrasting spikes beside rounded mounds. If you have plenty of space, plant in large drifts.

Astilbe in variety: their leaves are attractive too.

Cypripedium in variety: the hardy slipper orchids.

Dierama pendula: I have included these as they look particularly graceful arching over water and their reflection is pretty.

Gunnera manicata: a truly impressive foliage plant, best suited for a large pool and garden.

Hmerocallis in variety: the day lilies will thrive in a dry sunny border as well as in moist conditions.

Hostas in variety: fine foliage.

Iris kaempferi: the Japanese clematis flowered iris.

I. sibirica: marvellous value, with deep blue flowers.

Lysichitum americanum: yellow arum-like flowers.

L. camtschat cense.

Lythrum: the loose-strifes are striking flowers planted in a mass round a natural lake.

Miscanthus in variety: graceful perennial grasses.

Primulas in variety: do feed these with leaf mould or really old manure and plant them in bold drifts of one colour; discover which do well in lime and which prefer an acid soil.

Ranunculus aconitifolius flore pleno: some people call these Fair Maids of France, others Fair Maids of Kent or even White Bachelor's Buttons; they are a choice plant.

Rodgersia: these have giant chestnut-like leaves and feathery flowers.

Spiraea: the lovely, sweet smelling meadow sweet.

Trillium grandiflorum: for an acid soil when it will make a carpet.

Trollius in variety: commonly known as the globe flower, these are among the most beautiful of moisture-loving plants.

CHAPTER TEN

THE ROCK GARDEN

Rock gardens and alpine plants are so popular today that it is sometimes surprising to realize what a recent development they are in gardening history. Their story begins in the summer of 1777, when Sir Joseph Banks, naturalist and future President of the Royal Society, sailed to Iceland. Working with his librarian, the Swedish botanist Dr. Daniel Solander, he acquired one of the first extensive collections of Icelandic plants ever made and managed to bring most of them home successfully.

This expedition, however, is not of interest to the modern gardener for its botanical discoveries, but because during its course Banks made a twelve-day expedition to the summit of the volcano Hekla, for he was interested in the effects of its eruption five years previously. From the volcano's slopes he collected lava which was used as ballast for the ship on the return voyage. Once back in London Banks presented some of it to the Apothecaries' Garden at Chelsea, now called the Chelsea Physic Garden, where it was combined with forty tons of stone already acquired when major alterations had been made to the nine-feet-thick walls of the Tower of London. Together the lava and stone formed the framework of the first recorded rockery in England. To them were added flints, chalk and inevitably, broken London bricks. By all accounts, the result resembled more closely a heap of stone than an attractive background for plants growing in a natural manner—that would come later.

Early Rock Gardens

Although the rockery at the Chelsea Physic Garden was the first, it took less than fifty years for rockeries to become established as an almost essential feature for every garden. By the 1830s Jane and John Loudon, both prolific writers on all aspects of gardening, were writing articles about 'rockwork'. Indeed, in her first article on the subject, Jane Loudon was able to write, 'Everyone knows that rockwork is a collection of fragments of rock, stone, scoria from furnaces, and other substances thrown together in an artistic manner, so as to produce a striking and pleasing effect, and to serve as a nest or repository for the reception of Alpines and other dwarf plants.' She went on to say that, 'It may appear at first that as the collection of stones etc. is designed to appear wild and irregular, little Art would be required in its construction; but this is so far from being the case, that perhaps rockwork is more difficult to design and execute than any other kind of garden scenery.'

As we shall see, there was a great deal of truth in this. Jane Loudon considered Lady Broughton's rockwork at Hoole House near Chester to be the best rock garden in England. It was formed on a level surface and was an imitation of a Swiss mountain scene. To achieve the proper effect, the design required white stones, so large blocks of grey limestone were used, mingled with fragments of quartz, and white marble to simulate snow. Mrs. Loudon was quick to perceive that a 'single false step would have made the whole pass from the sublime to the ridiculous.' In her next article Mrs. Loudon describes a more natural rockwork, at Redleaf, near Penshurst in Kent the home of a Mr. Wells. The keynote of the design was the frequent outcropping of the rocky strata, simulating the character of the natural scenery around Tunbridge Wells, so that the gardener's artistry was given an advantage by its setting.

Mr. Wells's rockwork was quite different in character to Lady Broughton's. The existing scenery, complete with aged thorns and oaks remaining from a natural wood, made an admirable setting for the introduction of 'groups of rocks, not disposed according to any fixed plan, but they are intended to appear to rise out of the ground naturally'. To do this, a few stones were sunk into the ground, only just appearing above the surface, others then were half-visible, and above these others were jumbled together. At one moment in the description you might think that a modern rock garden was in the making, but further study and a glance at the illustrations reveals few plants and a 'picturesque mass of stones'. Moreover, in another part of this garden the remains of an old stone quarry was formed into a 'rocky hollow' with the rocks arranged to form beds for flowers which were mostly half-hardy, consisting of fuchsias, myrtles, and other greenhouse ornamental shrubs. And she continues: 'The rocky path, after leaving the hollow, conducts the stranger through the lawn, which is beautifully diversified with trees and rocks to the English flower garden.'

We can see from this that the early rock gardens might contain almost any species of plant. Indeed, although Lady Broughton's rockery included 'a collection of the most beautiful Alpine plants, particularly those of low growth', they were evidently not all true alpines, for Jane Loudon writes of retaining moisture 'around those plants which are liable to be injured by drought'. One of the most important features of any site for alpine plants is that it is well drained. In order to understand this early style of rock gardening, we must appreciate that in the first quarter of the nineteenth century, gardening was moving away from the open, airy landscape, familiar to us in the work of Capability Brown and Humphry Repton towards the High Victorian fashion for carpet bedding. Rock gardens were a part of this transformation: a new feature for gardens which were becoming, like the interiors of the houses they surrounded, increasingly cluttered.

A true Alpine garden, it should be understood, is a place where plants native to the Alps alone are grown. It should not be confused with a general rock-garden where we have mountain and other plants from the whole temperate world.

GERTRUDE JEKYLL 1901

Alpines

Although the cultivation of alpines was not always associated with rock gardens in the beginning, it soon came to be so. The spectacular scenery of Switzerland was enticing an ever-increasing flow of tourists, principally English ones, to the Alps. Here, in the foreground of magnificent views, they found in places that the ground was covered with exquisite flowering plants and evergreens. We can see from an early article written by 'An Amateur' on the 'Culture of Alpine Plants' in the May 1849 number of *The Horticultural Cabinet*, that the early attempts to grow these plants were not always successful. In England, he wrote, 'Alpine plants are often planted out on rockwork and in shady borders; but experience shows that they never succeed well or long in such situations; we therefore should endeavour to imitate their natural habits.' He suggests, instead, planting them in pots and over-wintering them in a frame, as good advice now as it was then for the high-altitude species. He defined alpines, incidentally, in the following manner: 'A collection of alpines properly consists of such plants as grow on high mountains, whether of this country, America, Switzerland or others. They are universally low, bushy, and mostly evergreen. In some of their native conditions they are covered with snow the greater part of the year...'

Clearly. by mid-century, the fashion was sending down its roots in just the same way as do the alpine plants. In 1859 Messrs. Backhouse of York, an illustrious nursery firm, made a rock garden in order that their customers might see and desire the special alpine plants that were available to them. Six years later they issued a long catalogue entirely devoted to alpine plants, a sure sign that these were in demand.

WILLIAM ROBINSON

On this wave of enthusiasm William Robinson, one of the most prolific gardening writers of the nineteenth century, published his book *Alpine Plants* in 1870, explaining in the intro-duction: 'This book is written to dispel a very general but erroneous idea, that the ex-quisite flowers of alpine region cannot be grown in gardens.' His reasons for recommending alpines are timeless. He includes them among the most beautiful flowers of northern, temperate regions saying that the amateur gardener 'might grow an abundance of them at a tythe of the expense required to fill a glass-house with costly Mexican or Indian orchids... In a word there is not a garden of any kind, even in the suburbs of our great cities, in which the flowers of alpine lands may not be grown and enjoyed.'

The site for the rock garden recommended by William Robinson is the same as one made today. It should be in an open situation, or one with 'bold prominence.' There should be no trees in or near the site because the roots would cause trouble and the shade cast would be detrimental as well as the dripping from the leaves. Robinson's whole advice is based on keeping a natural look, both in the choice of material and how the rocks are placed. His book is full of sound commonsense, not only about the construction of rock gardens but also about the care of plants right from propagation to plants in pots, watering and details of 'what to avoid'.

Robinson was often criticized as occasionally contentious and over-critical, but he did not hesitate to say what he thought: 'Few public gardens show worse examples of the traditional rockwork than Kew'. However, before you imagine that this is a criticism of the wonderful rock garden at Kew today, note that it was written twelve years before the present one was begun.

REGINALD FARRER AND E. A. BOWLES

Increasingly, the great rock gardeners were alpine specialists, far more interested in the plants than in the 'feature' that rockwork could provide. The two greatest names are those of Reginald Farrer and E.A. Bowles. Bowles, know as Gussie to his friends, was born in 1865 at Myddleton House, Enfield, where he lived and gardened all his life. He met Reginald Farrer, fifteen years his junior, in May 1910. This was the start of an important friendship. Both men were dedicated gardeners and both strongly attached to small alpine plants. On their plant-hunting expeditions together they found many treasures which they brought home to England and distributed liberally among their friends. Their first joint expedition together was to the Alps in June 1911 starting on Mont Cenis. They found huge drifts of *Anemone alpina* as well as rarities, and a new primula, to be called *P. bowlesia*. Bowles described it as an ugly duckling hybrid of *P. pedemontana*. It is hard to imagine that many plants escaped the combined eyes of these two men.

Reginald Farrer had already written a book on alpines and bog plants, *My Rock Garden* is full of criticism concerning the construction of rock gardens. 'Nature is never haphazard or chaotic—she may seem so, but she never is; and the rock garden which sincerely aims at following nature must have Nature's own unity and decision of purpose...The ideal rock garden must have a plan.' He says there are three prevailing plans none of which are good. The Almond Pudding scheme has spiky pinnacles of limestone inserted thickly with their points in the air; the Dog's Grave is a pudding shape but with the stones laid flat. The third style he called the Devil's Lapful, for it merely requires cartloads of bald square-faced boulders to be dropped about anywhere and plants placed between them. Clearly Farrer had no high opinion of rock gardening in the 1900s.

His ideal, he says, is to have an idea and to stick to it: 'Let the rock garden set out to be something definite, a feature of nature.' He mentions with praise the form of the glen at Kew and a gorge design at Warley Place, the home of the rich, eccentric, Miss Ellen Willmott, though he found it 'a trifle too violent to be altogether pleasant'. Clearly Farrer preferred writing about plants to the making of a rock garden. Like other writers on the subject he emphasizes the complete necessity of good drainage and of the correct placing of stones. 'Always set your rock with its largest surface to the ground,' he writes, and warns his readers to make sure that every nook between the stones is filled with soil so that roots penetrating below for moisture will not encounter a vacuum. He sees no advantage in keeping plants from the same country in the same place. 'Many plants—yes and many

'Phloxes smell to me like a combination of pepper and pig-stye...'

E.A. BOWLES, 1914.

Above: *Aquilegia alpina*, which, Reginald Farrer wrote 'always makes me feel quite gulpy'.

Left: The giant rockery at Swaylands, Penshurst, Kent in about 1906. Largely planted with spring flowers such as arabis, purple aubrieta, yellow alyssum and alpine phlox. Reginald Farrer would probably have included it in the category of rock garden he called the Devil's Lapful.

Left: Sir Frank Crisp's extraordinary rock garden at Friar Park, near Henley, Oxfordshire.

Right: Valerie Finnis's garden in Northamptonshire, showing raised beds for her rock plants.

alpines—are dowdy and plain. It is of no use to deny it. Their ugliness only adds to the beauty of their better favoured relatives...Certain flowers hold out the hand of comradeship. *Lilium rubellum* and *Aquilegia alpina* always make me feel quite gulpy.'

Above all, for Farrer, the rock garden 'is a place sacred to the brave little perennials of the mountain.' No lover of rock gardens should fail to read him. He has his own very personal style, and although opinionated, when he admires a plant or a situation he waxes eloquent, almost flowery. He was a great enthusiast.

A complete contrast to the serious, almost scholarly plantsmanship of Bowles and Farrer, is Frank (later Sir Frank) Crisp. No chapter on rock gardens, however brief would be complete without a mention of the extraordinary rock garden at his home at Friar Park, Henley, in Berkshire. Started in the 1890s it was a model of the Alps, with mountains high and low, gorges, valleys, passes, bridges, waterfalls, all represented with solid Yorkshire stones as the main structural ingredient. The plants were supplied by Messrs. Backhouse in the first instance and later by the Guildford Hardy Plant Co. He also made use of sham rock, which would sound unlikely if an article in the *Alpine Garden Society Bulletin* of June 1949 did not describe it. The artificial rocks were of 'half-dried concrete, given stratification marks by scoring them with a piece of broken wood, brushed over with a stable brush to give them a striated and slightly roughened surface dusted with sand and finished off with a spray of oxide of iron. When set they were ready for us.' There must always be a final 'cri de coeur'; in this case it was the herd of artificial chamois.

E. B. ANDERSON'S *THE SMALL ROCK GARDEN*

Before turning to more directly practical advice about rock gardening, there is one book you must not miss. This is *The Small Rock Garden* by E.B. Anderson, published in 1965. It is a storehouse of knowledge, easy to understand and with instructions which make one feel that the end result *can* be achieved. So often with 'instructive' books I turn the pages feeling it is all too complicated and difficult.

Anderson tells us that alpine plants are those that grow above where the trees end on the mountains, but that it is size and hardiness which determine what we grow in our rock gardens. He continues: 'In the small garden you will probably get more pleasure from this form of gardening than any other. Once you make acquaintance with them (rock plants), especially those of a more elfin beauty, they seat themselves firmly in your heart for ever.'

As for laying your stones, Anderson's advice is to pay a visit to a rock garden in your neighbourhood and learn from this how best to achieve a natural and telling effect. Obviously it is more economical to use local stone and it will never look out of place. Use stones of mixed sizes, none too heavy to handle yourself. Lay the broadest face downwards and ram soil very well round it so that the final result is complete stability which even your heaviest friend cannot disturb. Like others, he emphasizes the importance of filling the smallest crack with soil. To avoid another pitfall, make sure that you have no place in your rock bed where water will lie, unable to filter through. The test for this is to pour a gallon of water from a watering can on to a likely level position and you will soon find the answer. If the water does not percolate through quite quickly then the soil must be made more porous.

Modern Rock Gardening

Secretly, I do not wish to have a rock garden of my own. Growing alpines to perfection is a large subject in its own right, and I have never felt I could do it justice. This does not mean to say that I do not appreciate and love all those small flowers. There are however three rock gardens I know that I admire and in each of them alpine plants are the outstanding feature.

VALERIE FINNIS'S SLEEPER BEDS

The first is in Northamptonshire (alas too far away from my home in Gloucestershire to make it easy for me to visit often). Here a galaxy of alpine plants in raised beds are grown to perfection by that great gardener Valerie Finnis.

The beds are backed by a stone wall, and the front support is created by erstwhile railway sleepers—an ideal presentation for such plants, as they are high enough to be admired, touched, coddled and nurtured. An added advantage is that there is no need for dangerous walking across rocks or bending down to admire the smallest detail, as you are almost at eye level. There are no imitation Alps here or similar follies. It is an ideal home for plants and is one way in which I would enjoy growing alpine plants myself.

The area between the wall and the sleepers is filled with a mixture of loam, peat and grit in the proportion 2:1:1 to allow for good drainage. Most of the plants in these beds are hardy, but grown so that more delicate plants—such as the grey-leaf variety which need to be protected from too much rain—can be covered with glass or a cloche during the winter months. It is quite a good policy to gather all delicate plants together and put a glass light over them to simulate an unheated mini glass house. If need be, these lights can then be used for shading from the glare of the sun in summer.

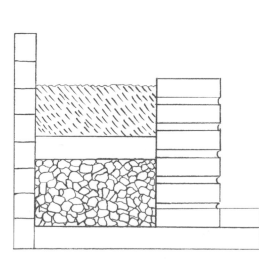 

Right: A two-deep sleeper bed constructed by Valerie Finnis.

Left: Cross section of a two-deep sleeper bed.
Fill as indicated.
1. Hardcore 9 in (23 cm)
2. Rough peat, compost etc. 3 in (7 cm)
3. 2 parts loam, 1 part peat and 1 part grit 6 in (15 cm)

Some of the advantages of raised beds are that you can incorporate specific mixtures for certain plants, it is easy to maintain a correct drainage system, and it is possible to sit on the edge of them while you work—as long as you can find a place not occupied by plants.

JOE ELLIOTT'S TROUGHS

Joe Elliott has lived with alpine plants all his life and you are immediately aware of this when you visit him and his nursery near Stow-on-the-Wold in Gloucestershire. His father Clarence Elliot, creator of the famous Six Hills Nursery in Hertfordshire, went on successful plant-hunting expeditions all over the world and brought back to England many new plants – *Thymus Hebrabarona* from Corsica and the almond-scented *Oxalis enneaphylla* from the Falkland Islands are only two of the many hundreds. But his chief innovation was growing alpines in stone sinks and farm troughs. He popularized the idea and made it possible for his customers to see and choose the troughs as well as their contents. During the 1930s he exhibited trough gardens at London's Chelsea Flower Show and Joe Elliott remembers making them up with a variety of plants and rocks—the latter being almost as important as the plants in an alpine-filled container.

Where do these troughs come from? Joe says that when he was a boy their house was always surrounded by sinks and troughs (some full others empty) which his father had found on farms. Today, you can use old stone kitchen sinks or even glazed porcelain ones that have been thrown out and replaced by stainless steel units, provided you cover the porcelain with hypertufa. After a short time this mixture weathers sufficiently to make

the porcelain look like stone.

To cover a porcelain sink, first scrub it thoroughly to get rid of any grease, then when it is dry, paint on a thin coat of bonding adhesive such as Unibond or Polybond. Make sure you apply this all over the surface then allow it to dry before sticking on the hyper-tufa. To make the hypertufa, you should have (by bulk) two parts of moistened sifted sphagum peat, one part of coarse sand or very fine grit, and one part of cement. Mix these together very thoroughly and, as you continue mixing, add water. Do not dilute too much. Your hypertufa should be solid enough to spread on to your sink, without sliding off. You do not need a thick layer, half an inch will be enough. There is no need to put the hypertufa on the inside of the sink, just put it low enough so that no white is showing when your new trough is filled with compost.

But before you fill it, decide where to put it. An open position is needed. Most alpines are sun lovers and all of them hate being dripped on from overhanging trees. They are small rather special plants, so do not hide them at the end of the garden but rather choose a spot near the house, such as the patio where you sit out on warm days. It is better to put troughs in a paved or gravel area, as if you set them in grass it makes for awkward mowing. If you have one trough, you are sure to want another, so bear this in mind when you are deciding where to put the first one. Joe Elliott has accumulated more than thirty over the years. He says, 'They line the edge of the wider paths, stand on paved areas or anywhere else where they fit in happily and appropriately. Each is a small rock garden with a few carefully chosen rocks which house an immense number of my favourite miniature plants.' I can see how alpines in troughs could well become an addiction.

Troughs in Joe Elliott's garden near Stow-on-the-Wold in Gloucestershire.

There are two vital points to remember. You must have adequate drainage holes and your troughs will look much better if they are raised off the ground. The ideal height for the top of the trough is 18 – 20 in (45 – 50 cm). They must be supported on a firm base, otherwise they will be top-heavy. The filling for your trough garden and the rocks you use will depend on your taste in plants, your locality and the availability of rock—as well as the amount of time you can spare for this type of gardening. A nursery which specializes in alpines will advise you as to soil, but let me repeat that alpine plants demand good drainage. You will soon be experimenting with different mixtures of leaf mould, loam, pea gravel, rock chippings, peat and coarse sand or grit. One of Joe Elliott's surprising but outstandingly successful ideas was to fill a stone-built raised bed with nothing but pea gravel (though with a dressing of bone- meal each spring). In the drought summer of 1976 almost all its inhabitants survived without once being watered during the rainless fifteen weeks.

I have talked about the raised beds made by Valerie Finnis. These were made against a wall, but free-standing raised beds constructed either of stone, wooden panels or brick are becoming more and more popular. The essential differences are, of course, their size and mobility. It is much easier to construct a large raised bed than to find a huge stone trough. Raised beds have space for more rampant rock plants and small shrubs than restricted troughs, so your thinking can be on a different scale. However, remember that troughs can be moved around but a raised bed is a permanent fixture. The important points they have in common are that they allow you to choose what soil mix you want, and they bring the plants closer to eye-level. These troughs and raised beds not only add to the aesthetic value of your garden, but they also make it possible to cultivate hundreds of plants in a restricted area. They can either be a focal point or create a pattern and you can site them so that you can walk from one to the other enjoying their individual character.

PENNY STRANGE'S SCREE BEDS

Another way of growing alpine plants is on a natural scree bed. This can be seen in another favourite garden of mine, Penny Strange's at Yew Tree Cottage, Ampney St. Mary, also in Gloucestershire. When Penny Strange came to live there about fourteen years ago, there was already a beautiful garden created and cared for by her mother. 'I love all small things,' says Penny, 'so naturally I wanted to grow small plants—alpines.' The only place left uncultivated by her mother was the over-large gravel drive. Many people might not have realized its potential, but fortunately Penny did. Now as you arrive at the cottage

The scree bed made on the driveway in Penny Strange's garden at her cottage in Gloucestershire

you are greeted, at any time of the year by a carpet of miniature plants, jostling one another for space, keeping out unwanted weeds, sometimes making a tapestry of colours and at others a complex of differing greens. Maybe I have made it sound big—it is not, but it is the home of hundreds of different plants.

To start the garden, the first thing Penny did was to make a collection of stones from the roadside and (with permission) from nearby fields. She then defined the outline of her new scree garden, for that is what it is, with a retaining wall only few inches high. She loosened the top few inches of what had once been part of the drive and infilled behind her wall with a mixture of compost, gravel and broken Cotswold stone. To this bone-meal was added, the only fertilizer it still gets annually each early spring. A flat look would have been unnatural and dull, so the surface was undulated slightly and a few larger stones were buried to at least half their depth. Many alpine plants love to be able to get their roots down and under stones to keep moist and cool.

While she was creating this new home for alpines she was busy reading *Collins Guide to Alpines* and as she said, 'I was becoming more and more hooked on them'. She joined the Alpine Garden Society and found their bulletins and seed catalogues invaluable. I know, though, that however much you read about plants you must see them growing before you realize their full potential and needs.

Once prepared, the area was given time to subside before planting. Penny went off with her lists of wants to recommended nurseries, coming home with quantities of container-grown plants, some of which were wrongly named though this has made her meticulous about accurate naming in her own nursery. Her new treasures were laid out in their pots and moved around until she felt she had achieved the best position, both for effect and the whims of her plants. Where height was needed she has put dwarf chamaecyparis and junipers. Useful broad-leafed evergreen are euonymus and small hebes, lavenders and euryops. Natural hangers or fallers over walls include aubrieta, arenaria, rock phlox, *Silene maritima*, and many of the thymes. Useful infillers are low campanulas, camomile, *Viola cornuta*, mossy saxifrage and alpine erinus.

In her opinion, the best foliage plants she grows for year long effect are sempervivums, dwarf *Berberis thunbergii*, especially 'Atropurpura nana', *Hebe* 'E.B. Anderson' and *H. pinguifolia* 'Pagei', the encrusted saxifrage and Kabscia varieties, erodiums, small sedums, the small grey- leafed achilleas, and another grey treasure, *Tanacetum densum* (sometimes erroneously called *Chrysanthemum haradjanii*).

Left: *Aubrieta deltoides* 'Godstone'.

Right: *Thymus drucei*. Ideal plants for falling over walls on the edge of a raised bed.

Some of Penny Strange's star performers:
Opposite top: *Saxifraga oppositifolia.*
Opposite bottom: *Violo cornuta.*
This page top: *Anemone blanda* 'White Splendour'.
Bottom right: *Aquilegia bertolonii.*

A useful foliage plant, the grey treasure *Tanacetum densum.*

Above: A raised stone bed at Frank Cabot's Stone Crop Nurseries, Cold Springs, New York, consisting solely of cut tufa and tufa rubble with *Saxifragia kabschia* on the bed.

In my garden, I have not so far succeeded with that gem *Tropaeolum polyphyllum*, but Penny has, probably because she paid more attention than I did when she planted it, giving it a well-drained root run in a peaty soil. It is the initial moment of getting this member of the nasturtium family established that is important; once on its way it will ramp. I wonder why Penny thinks of *Convolvulus cneorum* as a foliage plant, its glistening white flowers are always what catch my attention. She favours two variegated leafed genera, grasses and thymes. *Carex firma* 'Variegata' makes neat tufts with spiky leaves, while the pretty variegated thymes, especially 'E.B. Anderson' and 'Doone Valley', are mild spreaders.

Generally speaking I do not like plant lists in books, I always think it is easier to turn to a catalogue; but even so I am going to give Penny's short list of her star performers in this alkaline scree bed over the years:

Anemone blanda 'White Splendour'
Aquilegia bertolonii
A. akitensis
A. viridiflora
Arenaria montana
Campanula x *haylodgensis*
Crepis incarnata
Diascia 'Ruby Field'
Dianthus freynii
Erodium macredenum
Geranium sanguinem 'Lancastriensis'
G. x 'Ballerina'
Geum borisii
Hacquetia epipactis
Helichrysum milfordiae
Origanum laevigatum
Pusatilla vulgaris
Saxifraga oppositifolia
Sisyrinchium macounii
Veronica 'Blue Tit'
Viola cornuta
Viola glabella

'If any success in the cultivation of rock-plants is expected, it is only reasonable to suppose that one must take the trouble to learn something about the plants, their kinds and their needs, and it is equally necessary to take the trouble to learn how their places are to be prepared.'

GERTRUDE JEKYLL.

These gardens are all on approximately the same latitude and all in the same country. In the USA, these three different types of alpine garden can all be seen on the East Coast at the newly established Stone Crop Nurseries at Cold Springs, New York. Here visitors can see well-established plants in ideal surroundings and can obtain advice based on years of practical experience. As we saw from the history of rock gardening, alpines can be difficult to grow and local conditions are important. If you want to succeed with them, therefore, do not hesitate to seek advice from specialist nurseries. Remember, too that no matter where you live almost every botanic garden in the world has a rock garden of some kind, so there will always be the 'right' place to visit to find ideas for planting. The rock garden at Kew is now more than an acre in size. Constructed on a level site, it has so many different aspects and conditions that lessons can be learnt by anyone visiting it. The New York Botanic Garden has a large-scale rock garden, supervized by experts and the work augmented with the help of volunteers. (The latter give their time free in return for the experience and knowledge they acquire. This is a wonderful and practical idea both for the garden and for the volunteers.) Even if you live in a hot climate there are equivalents. What are the extraordinary cactus gardens, but rock gardens using succulents instead of alpines?

A retaining wall bed in bloom at Stone Crop Nurseries.

Left: The Thompson Memorial Rock Garden at the New York Botanical Garden. *Right:* In a hot climate succulents are the equivalents of alpines. Here they make a striking display in the cactus garden at the Huntington Botanic Garden, California.

CHAPTER ELEVEN

GARDEN ORNAMENT

'Every straight walk ought to have an appropriate termination...Vases, statues, seats, alcoves...will give sufficient obstruction to the end of a walk.'

EDWARD KEMP, 1864.

Ornament, whether a simple painted seat or a costly summer house, provides an important attraction in any garden. The essential rule is that its scale must always relate to its site. After this you should remember that natural materials are nearly always more pleasing to the eye and the touch than synthetic ones, that local materials—pine wood in conifer country, limestone in limestone country—will never look out of place, and that if you muddle together objects from extravagantly different periods you may be thought a little eccentric by your visitors, although there is a fine precedent for this in eighteenth-century parks and, anyway, you can reassure yourself that conformity leads swiftly to dull regimentation.

Garden ornament has such a long and varied history that I can only extract a few favourite examples and lay them out, like a soldier with his kitbag, for inspection. In the parks and gardens which you visit you will find your own likes and dislikes such as a perfectly proportioned classical urn or an angular bench design...Look for them and decide whether they will fit your garden design and your budget and then see if you can find, make, or have made something similar. Occasionally, you will see some object, as I have done, which will fire your imaginaton with ideas for planting designs: an old sundial ideal for the centre of a herb garden, a stone bench which will make the perfect focal point at the end of a walk, or even an ordinary wooden tub bound with metal bands. If it is a bargain, or if you think it might be one, or if you hope it could be—do not hesitate, buy it. You are unlikely to regret it.

'Roosting Places' to Temples

One of the last true follies to be made in the British landscape was Lord Berners's folly near Faringdon in Oxfordshire. Completed in 1935 after tremendous local opposition, it is now largely obscured by trees but has a fine outlook on the surrounding countryside.

By and large, however, such extravagance is outside the scope of most modern gardeners. As with the grand country houses of the eighteenth and nineteenth centuries, we can only look back nostalgically on the breadth of vision, which went with the depth of pocket, that permitted their construction.

Much earlier, in the Tudor age, we find ideas mentioned which are more in keeping with the scope of our ambitions today. Although there were proper buildings, such as small banqueting rooms and gazebos, like those at Montacute, there were also charming features on a smaller scale. When, in 1521, Henry VIII confiscated Thornbury Castle in Gloucestershire from the Duke of Buckingham, whom he then had executed, his commissioners reported that in the orchard there were 'many goodly allies to walk in openly; and round about the same orchard is covered on a good height, other goodly allies with roosting places covered thoroughly with white thorn and hazell'.

'Roosting places' is a descriptive phrase which immediately brings to mind the image of a couple sitting on a bench in the privacy of a covered alleyway. Like the covered seat described in Chapter Four, 'The Herb Garden', the roosting place is as much an excuse for something to grow climbing plants up as it is a garden building. A seat of this sort is a charming, impermanent structure—more part of an alley, fence or wall than a true garden house.

There is no better account of the reasons for having a summer house in the garden than John Rea's suggestions for a 'Somer-house', written in 1665. 'It will be required to have in the middle of one side of this Flower-garden a handsome Octangular Somer-house, roofed every way, and finely painted with Landskips, and other conceits, finished with seats about, and a table in the middle; which serveth not only for delight and enter-tainment, to sit in, and behold the beauties of the flowers, but for many other necessary purposes...for writing the names, both in planting and taking up, of all flowers...for shelter, in case of a sudden shower of rain; and divers other purposes that it cannot (with any con-venience) be wanting, and therefore ought to be considered in the setting up of the walls, wherein it is to be placed, so that it come not further into the garden, than the just breadth of the border, for putting of it out of square.'

John Rea's emphasis on usefulness went out of fashion in the following century. All sorts of garden ornament, but principally buildings and monuments, appeared as eye-catchers—points to walk to, turn around and discover yet another vista through the groves. Today, as we visit the famous gardens of this era we enjoy these ornaments. Chiswick, Rousham, Stowe and Stourhead, Hagley, Studley Royal and Castle Howard, Blenheim,

Every gardener should keep an eye open for interesting features in other gardens, such as these seats in the Abbey Gardens, Bury St. Edmund's, Suffolk or the classical urn glimpsed at Millmead, Bramley, Surrey where Gertrude Jekyll and Edwin Lutyens designed the garden.

Below: A monument-filled landscape at Shugborough in Staffordshire, typical of the eighteenth-century love of ruins, painted by Nicholas Dall.

The Hermit's Cell at Badminton,
Avon, designed by Thomas
Wright for Charles, 4th Duke of
Beaufort in 1750.

Kew and Painshill—all great names and all containing temples, pagodas, obelisks, pavilions,
bridges, grottoes, alcoves, ruins and archways by the famous architects and designers of
the day from Flitcroft and Hawksmoor to Chambers and the great William Kent. The
origin of these 'ornaments' was often in fantasy—think of the hermits' cells and root
houses—yet they were always carefully placed, as though the landscape was a stage set.

Although most present-day private gardens are too small to accommodate a temple
or an obelisk, we can learn a great deal from this theatrical approach as well as from study-
ing the proportions of the buildings and some of the minor incidents. The pretty arbours
at Rousham could well become a pattern for one in a modern garden. At Barnsley, we
borrowed the idea of trellis work arbours from those at Villandry, and though they will
not last for ever, they have already given us several years enjoyment as, each summer, they
become covered with golden hops and vines.

Twenty years ago we were *given* a small temple building from nearby Fairford Park.
It dates from about 1770 and was probably designed by Eames, a follower of Capability
Brown. The cost of moving and re-erecting it seemed ridiculously extravagant at the time,
but it has proved a tremendous addition to the garden, worth the cost many times over.
Many years ago the garden designer Percy Cane advised me to try to use the longest vista
to the best advantage and so we placed the temple at one side, looking across the whole
breadth of the garden. The effect was to make the garden feel much larger than it is—
a purely theatrical device.

Choosing a Summer House

Unless you too are lucky enough to be given a summer house, you must build one. Even
a small summer house made with local stone or brick will be expensive, but if well designed
will probably never be regretted for its usefulness and beauty. If you are not a professional,
or even an amateur builder, then you must find someone to help you who knows what
he or she is doing. Badly made small buildings can quite easily collapse as a result of
hard frosts or even gale-force winds.

If you are prepared to go to the expense of having a small summer house built, then
you will find that nineteenth- and twentieth-century gardening books are crammed with
ideas.

Typical garden buildings of the last century can be seen in books by John B. Papworth, Humphry Repton, John and Jane Loudon and Shirley Hibberd. The buildings fitted
the scale of the gardens , which once again were smaller, with flowers brought back
to borders round the house and also the villa gardens of the new middle class citizens
created as a result of the Industrial Revolution.

Papworth's conservatory is 'a very desirable appendage to the mansion itself...indeed,
it presents such an endless source of amusement at all seasons that its frequent adoption
may be well expected'. His design for 'A Garden Seat' is perhaps grander than anything
we might immediately consider. 'The construction,' he says, 'is very simple, consisting
of oak pillars and iron rods to form the arcades and trellises'. The handyman gardener could
use this design modified, as a pattern and grow vines and other climbers round the pillars.

In *Rustic Adornments for Homes of Taste* Hibberd gives several ideas for summer houses
with quite detailed instructions for making them. They are typical of mid-nineteenth-century
style and many of them would not blend with twentieth-century architecture.

Later books by and about garden designers such as William Mawson, Harold Peto,
Guy Dauber, and of course Sir Edwin Lutyens contain a wealth of possibilities.

When you are choosing a design and a builder has told you it is possible to construct it, repeat to yourself and to him the following principles. A summer house should
not only be attractive to look at but be comfortable to sit in. It should serve the purpose
of shading you from the hot sun and at the same time allow eough light to enter so that
you can read with ease. It should provide shelter from the prevailing wind, but also allow
a good view of the garden.

The Lutyens summer house at Millmead, Bramley in Surrey is one of my favourites.
It is both simple and beautiful; fits perfectly into the garden and is in keeping with the
house. Another favourite is the circular garden house built a few years ago in Hardy Amies's
garden. In this small garden there are no trees, so the building acts as shade as well as providing a focal point at the end of a central path leading from the house.

A rustic summer house from
Shirley Hibberd's *Rustic
Adornments for Homes of Taste*
(1856).

The circular garden house in
Hardy Amies's garden at Langford
in Oxfordshire.

Grottoes

Grottoes go back to the earliest gardens where they were sacred caves, the homes of the water nymphs. Classical Roman gardens had them and they were important features in Renaissance Italian gardens when water effects such as fountains and hidden sprays were the height of fashion.

In England one of the earliest grottoes was made at Enstone in Oxfordshire by Thomas Bushell, at one time secretary to Francis Bacon, who had a passion for philosphy. His grotto became so famous that even King Charles I visited it in 1643. There were water jokes such as cocks which could be turned to make a canopy of falling water to soak the imprisoned visitor if he attempted to escape. Sadly Bushell's garden has disappeared but pictures of the grotto and fountains can be seen in *Plots Natural History of Oxfordshire*.

Pope finally set the fashion for grottoes in England when, between 1720 and 1725, he made one in his grounds at Twickenham. It is a cleverly devised subterranean passage connecting two parts of his garden. Pope described it as a luminous room, 'finished with shells and interspersed with pieces of looking-glass in angular forms…when a lamp is hung in the middle, a thousand pointed rays glitter and are reflected over the place'. Strangely, at this time, Pope was attacking the formal, artificial garden, although his grotto had both these qualities. It took several years for grottoes to change and become dramatic natural caves composed of rugged fallen rocks. Whatever their character they were always the place for contemplation.

Grottoes have been out of favour with gardeners for a hundred years or more. The Victorians thought them disagreeable and injurious to health. Now, however, they are coming back into fashion.

A grotto which until recently has been ignored is the one in the grounds of Marlborough College in Wiltshire. It was made by Lady Hertford in the 1730s built into the side of a Neolithic mound. Lady Hertford described it as being newer and prettier than Pope's. I can only describe it to you as it appears today, for the Hertfords left Marlborough in 1750 and no more was heard of the grotto. It became a bothy for the gardeners, where they could sit and keep their tools. Now through the inspiration of Diane Reynell and the fine wormkanship, imagination and research of Simon Verity this grotto is once more coming to life. The wooden doors have been opened and will soon be removed, the sun reflects into a small circular pool at the entrance and throws light onto the vaulted ceiling of the central semi-circular apse. Water will flow from a niche at the back falling into a huge clam shell. The walls are made of flint, encrusted with Ormer shells from the Channel Islands and a beautiful, shining blue vitrous material, the waste from an eighteenth-century ironworks. It was the same blue used at Claremont and by Kent at Chiswick. There are oyster shells and Bristol diamonds, a red sandstone matrix with quartz crystals. By tradition this is the birthplace of Merlin, and here wonders never cease.

A modern romantic grotto was recently made at Bradley Court, a beautiful seventeenth-century house in Gloucestershire. A dead elm was felled and when its huge roots were removed a vast hole set Andy Garnet thinking and his imagination working. It was at the end of a long grass vista, beyond a statue backed by evergreen bushes. The statue could well be the final event but now for the observant a surprise awaits them. A path winds its way ever deeper and deeper through hollies and privets and ferns, getting darker as apparently the path moves downwards into the womb of the earth. It is, in a way, an illusion of descent, for the soil displaced by the falling tree was used to mound up the sides, thereby creating natural walls through which you wind until finally you reach the inside of the grotto with its caving roof, skillfully constructed with the help of Andy's engineering brain. Water drips continuously into a shallow pool before running further on its natural course. Enough light streams through a central ceiling cavity to bring life to the water and green to the hart's tongue ferns which burst from the crevices.

A grotto revival may be in its infancy. Certainly, eighteenth-century grottoes are receiving more attention and care than they have done for years.

One could spend weeks discovering grottoes throughout the country, for there are many of them. In the eighteenth century there were even grotto makers, the most renowned of whom were Joseph and Joshua Lane, who made many of the famous grottoes which can still be seen today: at Stourhead, Bowood and Wardour Castle in Wiltshire and Wycombe Abbey in Buckinghamshire. One of the finest grottoes still existing, but less well-known than those by the Lanes, is at Goldney House, Clifton, Bristol. It is a perfect work of artificial delight and you should try to see it if you can.

Garden Furniture

Compared with other garden features, garden furniture such as chairs, benches and tables seems to have been neglected by the early gardeners, and it was not until the sixteenth century that outdoor furniture appears in the garden scene. In medieval pictures, the days of the flowery mead, the garden occupants looked as though they were happy sitting on a grassy bank enjoying the sunshine and flowers. Perhaps the ladies' voluminous skirts protected them from the damp grass, but I felt sympathy towards the young men with scant skin-tight pants.

'To see urns, obelisks and waterfalls laid open; the nakedness of our beloved mistresses, the Naiads and the Dryads exposed by that ruffian Winter to universal observaton, is a severity scarcely to be supported by the help of blazing hearths, cheerful companions, and a bottle of most grateful burgundy.'
WILLIAM SHENSTONE, c. 1745.

'Gardens are made to sit in.'
THOMAS D. CHURCH, 1955.

Indoor furniture was simple and utilitarian and the housewife might have carried a wooden bench outside when the sun was shining but the natural place to sit was either on the ground, a low bank or mound and these developed into turf covered benches with wooden or brick sides. These benches are really only an extension of the idea of raised beds, which I have described in Chapter Six, 'Beds and Borders'. The obvious place to have a turf bench would be against a wall or palisade, protected against the wind and with a ready-made backrest. Not much imagination would be required to do this and it would incorporate a new element into the garden.

By Tudor times when great importance was set upon aromatic plants and herbs, camomile-covered seats became the fashion. These are easy to copy in or beside your own herb garden, using a simple framework of bricks or planks infilled with soil. The two important points to remember are to make the sides strong and solid so when heavy people sit down these do not bow outwards, and then you must firm the infilling soil down extremely well before doing any planting, otherwise as it settles it will sink and become an uncomfortable seat.

A seat like this can be made much more attractive if it has some sort of arch or bower, however simple, over it as described in Chapter Four, 'The Herb Garden'.

As this is the kind of bench you will use mostly in the summer, it is a practical thought to have climbers over it. Choose those which need hard pruning each winter, then if repairs are needed to the trellis it can easily be done without hurting the climbers after these have

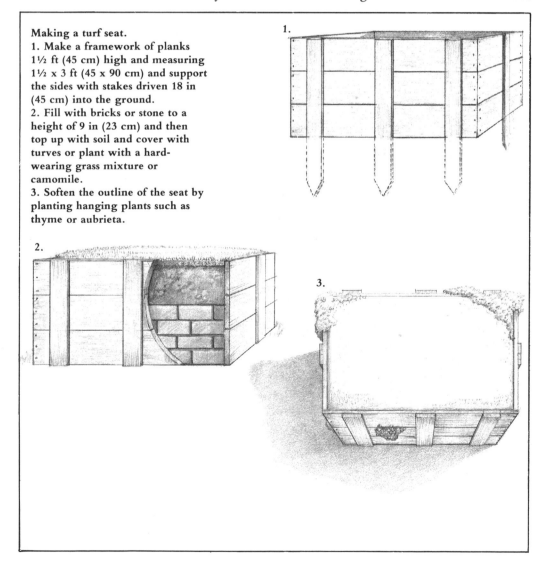

Making a turf seat.
1. Make a framework of planks 1½ ft (45 cm) high and measuring 1½ x 3 ft (45 x 90 cm) and support the sides with stakes driven 18 in (45 cm) into the ground.
2. Fill with bricks or stone to a height of 9 in (23 cm) and then top up with soil and cover with turves or plant with a hard-wearing grass mixture or camomile.
3. Soften the outline of the seat by planting hanging plants such as thyme or aubrieta.

A medieval manuscript
illumination showing turf seats
round the garden, raised beds and
trellis-work.

A three-sided fifteenth-century
turf bench in use.

Even the simplest seat looks beautiful covered by an arbour. This painted wooden seat at Shugborough, Staffordshire was sheltered by the weeping branches of a Camperdown Elm.

been pruned. Golden hop, *Humulus lupulus aureus*, makes a tremendous amount of growth each summer and has the prettiest of hops by the autumn. *Vitis vinifera* 'Brandt' or *V.c. purpurea* both have attractive leaves and also bunches of grapes, decorative rather than useful. Treat the hop as herbaceous, cutting it to ground level in the winter and prune the vines hard. You could also use annual climbers such as sweet peas, *Cobaea scandens, Maurandia erubescens* and *Tropaeoleum canariensis*. I believe that ivies would be too heavy and would need a more permanent fixture.

John Worlidge, that most practical writer in the period after the Restoration of Charles II in 1660, has useful thoughts. 'For cool recesses in the hottest times, it hath been useful to erect or frame arbours with poles or rods.' However, he does not altogether recommend them as the seats 'are apt to be moist'. And, 'If the weather invite you to sit in the air, a seat under the shade of some platanus, Lin-Tree is much more pleasant than to be hood-winked in an arbour.' You may choose a seat which can be moved about the garden, 'This seat may be made close behind, that being set with the back to the wind, will be both warm and dry'. A niche in the wall is a good place: 'at the ends of your walks are the most proper plces for such seats, that whilst you sit in them you have the view of your garden.'

Worlidge's thoughts are the forerunners of the eighteenth-century temples, for he describes and recommends semi-circular seats with a cupola, a wall behind and three or four columns in front. As for colour, they may be 'painted with a white colour in Oyl, or as best pleases your fancy.'

In the nineteenth century garden seats became important, for all the writers have something to say about them. Jane Loudon remarks that seats for a garden or pleasure ground are usually bought ready-made. A pleasant idea is to have one which is movable, to wheel about from one place to another. On a terrace, seats should be erected at each end, made of wood and of a 'somewhat massive design'. A novel suggestion was to paint the seat white and whilst the paint was still tacky to strew very fine sand on to it 'which will make it a very good imitation of stone'. Probably not very practical as I believe this would gather the dirt quite quickly. True to Victorian romantic thought, Mrs. Loudon wrote, 'Agreeable variety may be occasionally produced by having the stump of an old tree formed into a seat and twining ivy and creeping flowers round it.'

Regarding the question of what colour seats should be—natural wood, stained or painted—Charles M'Intosh decreed in 1853 that 'All garden seats except the rustic, should be painted stone-colour, as harmonizing better with vegetation than any other colour, and of all colours the most unfit for the purpose is green.' Shirley Hibberd in 1870 wrote, 'Wood in its natural colour is much to be preferred to painted wood. The feet of all chairs should be touched with hot pitch sufficient to make the whole impervious to moisture.'

As one would expect Gertrude Jekyll has useful comments. She tells us that teak and oak are the best materials to use, I wonder whether she knew about the wood iroko, imported today, which is not so durable as teak but takes on a very attractive silvery hue as it weathers. She comments, 'Green is a doubtful colour, as it is likely to quarrel with the varied natural greens which are near it. White is safe, but looks rather staring during the seasons when there is no brilliant colour in the garden to relieve it.' In my opinion a very deep green, so dark you have to look twice before you realize it is not black, is very chic, especially for tubs. It is a safe colour to use in almost all circumstances. I first saw this in a garden of great taste in the south of France.

Colours, of course, look different and have a different impact according to their surroundings. In warm sunshine the blue-green used by Lawrence Johnstone in his French garden near the Mediterranean coast looks smart and right, and it can look good in many English gardens although I believe a warmer colour should be used where the natural colour of the stone is dark and cold. The Lawrence Johnstone blue-green came from the glaze of that colour in china pots which were in his French garden. A few years ago, walking in this garden one could see fragments of the toolshed door and other pieces which bore traces of this colour. He deliberately used it to blend with the foliage. You may visit Hidcote in Gloucestershire and see the same colour on the tubs and old stable doors (now part of the shop) and then go to nearby Snowshill where the woodwork is painted 'Wade Blue'. Although the original 'Wade Blue' had lead in it, now it is no longer an ingredient and the colour is subtly different.) Jim Marshall of the National Trust tells me that Lawrence Johnstone used white, matt black and dark green for the Hidcote garden furniture. Who, one asks, is the arbiter of taste?

'The choice of garden seats, as well as the spot on which to place them, requires a degree of taste and judgement apparently seldom bestowed on the subject...rustic seats should be confined to rustic scenery; and the seats for a lawn ought to be of comparatively simple and of architectural forms.'

CHARLES M'INTOSH, 1853.

Writers have always disagreed on the correct colour for garden seats. Although white-painted furniture can distract attention from the rest of the garden, it is particularly suitable for well-designed seats on open lawns.

With a background of red brick, seats can be painted white, grey or the deep green mentioned before. There is plenty of scope for choosing interesting, warm colours provided they blend with or complement their surroundings. I am all for experimenting and finding an original idea. However, whatever your choice, a seat should always give the impression of being there to be sat on and, as Miss Jekyll says, 'That is not likely to be very convincing if there is no path to give access to it'.

There is much to be said for estate colours, that is for doorways and railings of cottages belonging to an estate all to have the same colour. This creates a continuity and meaning. It is an idea which influenced us in choosing the colour for our iron railings and gates in the garden. We were having much difficulty in making a decision and then saw the dark blue which is used at Badminton. This decided us, and we have used this colour ever since. As with many colours it looks rather strong when first painted but soon weathers to a more mellow shade. Nonetheless, though I like it on the gates and railings, I would not want it for the seats.

Beautiful seats have been made of stone, one sees these in photographs of Edwardian gardens where they were added more for ornament than use, making part of a grand stone terrace or stairway. Probably they were not sat on for too long except in the height of summer, for they are cold and uncomfortable. However, they are ideal for a pause and

give solidity to a garden. Remarkably good reproductions are made by both Chilstone of Newport Pagnell and by Haddonstone of East Haddon in Northamptonshire. Several years ago, we bought two and these are now indistinguishable from real stone. My favourite is slightly curved and one of the lions which form the supports has a covering of moss over his feet as though it were a shawl.

There are pretty wrought iron seats in eighteenth-century garden illustrations and then in the next century when cast iron became the fashion, seats, tables, urns and all sorts were turned out in quantity for the Victorian garden. The seat illustrated by William Robinson in 1868 is surprisingly comfortable as the flexible strips of metal give way gently as you sit on them and almost mould themselves to your shape. The use of cast iron opened the way to making seats and tables with many decorative patterns and these you can see in gardens today. They always add a touch of style. Maybe they are hard to sit on and unless kept well painted Charles M'Intosh's remark of 1853 is as true today as it was then: 'The only objection urged against them is oxidation, which is apt to spoil ladies' dresses.' Even so, I would rather have them made of the real thing than modern plastic which, by pretending to be something it is not, looks ugly.

Elegant iron-work makes attractive seats which are easy to move. The seats of the chairs are made of flexible metal strips which give way gently as you sit on them.

So for the garden maker today what are the choices? There are good reproductions made of the nineteenth-century iron furniture, which should be durable and heavy in weight but not in style. I believe there is scope for an enterprizing production of metal garden furniture, as long as it is practical, comfortable and beautiful. Stone benches are being reproduced, and in the garden they are admirable for a focal point where the sitter will not linger too long, and in order to get them naturally weathered as fast as possible they should be under a tree where they will get dripped on regularly. As for wooden seats, these range in quality and price from craftsman-made to cheap substitutes which will quickly deteriorate. For years Lister's teak seats have held the market and are still as good as ever, but now is the time to look around and select from other collections. Chatsworth Carpenters have elegant designs of chairs, tables and tubs, and Andrew Grace of Much Hadham, Hertfordshire constructs gazebos in which to put the benches and seats he also makes. Charles Verey designs for Green Bros. of Hailsham in Sussex who also make replicas of the beautiful seats designed by Sir Edwin Lutyens. The satisfaction of their design has stood the test of time. If you make a visit to Hidcote and nearby Snowshill, the home of the late Charles Wade, to note the two different blues used on the woodwork, you could also notice the

Snowshill 'Conversation Seat' made by Charles Verey.

very attractive 'Conversation Seat' made recently by Charles Verey especially for Snowshill. It is comfortable, has flowing lines and as its name implies is suitably shaped for talking.

Pots and Tubs

If you go into a garden, large or small and there are pots and tubs about overflowing with flowers you may be sure that the owner is a plant lover—not, of course, if there is one sickly geranium surrounded by lobelia, only half filling the container, but if there are flowers of all sorts spilling out generously. Pots and tubs fall into two categories: those which can be easily moved about and grouped together to create a display in the summer and larger containers which because of their weight become permanent or semi-permanent features.

It is lovely to see beautiful old pots like the one in the centre of the White garden at Sissinghurst and the terracotta basket-weave pots on the garden stairs at Powis Castle. Then on holidays in countries such as Spain, or Italy we have all seen attractive terracotta pots for sale and wondered at their cheapness—if only we could get them home. Once when driving our car through Tuscany we bought four large terracotta pots and these became our hand luggage. They have lived ever since on our verandah, refilled twice a year with appropriate goodies.

Permanent urns provide a magnificent feature at Stourhead, Wiltshire.

Fortunately, a wide selection of containers is now available closer to home. There are several good pot-throwers who exhibit their wares at Chelsea and other flower shows. If you want their addresses you can get these by writing to the Royal Horticultural Society, Vincent Square, London SW1 (Enclose a SAE!). We have a talented local potter, David Garland, in nearby Chedworth whose workshop is full of original and interesting containers. Both Chilstone and Haddonstone have taken great trouble in finding and reproducing old patterns of urns, pots and jardinières so it is not necessary to be content with inferior work. Some of the reconstructed stone ones are dreadful, especially those made mainly with cement mix which gives an unattractive, artificial texture.

Top right and left: Pots and tubs are a useful means of altering the focus of a garden. In these two photographs we can see how they have been added to emphasize the outline of a path.
Above: The massive use of oranges and palm trees standing out for the summer in the garden beside the orangerie at Versailles.

Buying pots is a much cheaper occupation than putting up a garden temple or even buying a statue, but the fun of filling them is matched by the pleasure of finding homes for them around the garden. Pots, urns and tubs can mark the entrance to a pathway, give a demarcation line between lawn and terrace. You may stand them at the top and bottom of a garden stairway and flank the sides of a path. Terraces usually demand them and so does your patio where you sit in the evening. They always look right beside a formal pool and of course geraniums or pelargoniums in pots look wonderful on the steps leading up to your sitting room door. A gap through a wall can be made more interesting by 'stepping' the wall and standing pots on it and an urn on a plinth gives immediate height where it is needed in a design and acts as a focal point.

When you have decided on your sites start keeping your eyes open for the right containers, making sure that their size is relative to the surroundings. Something too small will look insignificant and anything too large will be overpowering—I believe it is better to err on the large side when in doubt. Consider the wind problem, remembering that a strong unruly gust can quickly destroy many months' plant growth in a container, so here is the place for an urn, statue or obelisk. (Obelisks need not be as large as they were in eighteenth-century landscapes!) Near the house you will want to use scented plants and should attend to detail; the bolder arrangements should go where they will be viewed from a distance.

Near the house and in small gardens, pots should be moved around frequently so they will always look their best, in fact they should be treated more as flower arrangements. There are two places in our garden where I use them like this, one is by our kitchen door and there is always a supply of cooking herbs, and the other is on our drawing-room steps which lead straight into the garden.

Filling Pots and Tubs

WINTER PLANS

The amount of plants you put in will obviously relate to the inside measurement of the container and how much soil it will hold. We usually completely change the soil when we prepare the winter tubs, using our own homemade compost fortified with peat and a slow-release fertilizer. On our terrace we have four 27 in (75 cm) diameter half barrels with holes drilled in their bottoms for drainage. When these arrive (costing about £12/$18) they have a strong aroma of whisky or brandy which gives confidence that the wood is well treated and that they will last for years. I recommend them, but remember that the bottoms of wooden containers should not be on the ground—½ in (12 mm) gap for air circulation will increase their life considerably.

As the winter arrangement will last from October until middle or late May, (in fact more than half the year), much thought should be devoted to how they are filled. This is the routine. First choose a not-too-tall standard for the centre; holly, box, osmanthus, euonymus, variegated rhamnus or any evergreen which has a good shape and stands 2½ – 3¼ ft (75 – 100 cm) tall. These are plants which will be used later in the garden and whilst they are growing on they are serving a useful purpose. Having half filled the container, stand the chosen evergreen in the centre at the correct height on the soil, but at this stage do not infill round it. Instead start planting round it in layers.

Thinking of successive flowering, nothing is more cheering for you and the bees than a display of early crocus in February and March. They will open and close according to the sunshine. Then the hyacinths will flower in April, followed by tulips in May. When planting these start with the tulips as the deepest layer; the bulbs are 10 in (25 cm) from the height of the rim of the barrel, twelve at least and concentrated nearer the centre than the outside. Then add a sprinkling of compost, but just allow the tips of the tulips to show so that when you add the next layer, which is of hyacinths, they do not overlay the tulips. Concentrate twelve of these on the outside and slightly intermingle with the tulips. Then add more compost, covering the whole barrel leaving about 3 – 4 in (7 – 10 cm) for the next layer. Next lay out twenty-five crocuses and between them put some low evergreen such as winter-flowering pansies, saxifrage, teucrium, arabis, aubrieta, probably four of two varieties so they make a green impact during the winter and will give a spasmodic flowering. Finally, before filling the containers with soil to the rim, add some small-leafed ivy or periwinkles to fall down the sides. This may seem a lot in a small space, but they will make an impact. As they should all be taken out after seven months to make way for the summer flowers, they do not have time to become overcrowded.

This winter our terracotta 'hand luggage' pots from Tuscany have 18 in (46 cm) variegated box as central features surrounded by *Viola labradorica* and hyacinths called 'amethyst'. I once read that hyacinths look out of place in a garden except near a building. Whether right or wrong, I have kept to this philosophy and plant them chiefly in tubs, or beds by the house.

SUMMER PLANS

Towards the end of May, a day comes when these containers are past their best—the last tulip has faded and summer is in the air. Everything is taken out, the bulbs put to dry, and the plants dug into spare places in the garden; the central features are kept for another year. Leave as much soil as possible in the barrels as they should have had a complete change in the autumn. The central feature is the lemon-scented verbena *Lippia citriodora* grown as standards. Surround these with the ivy leaf 'Ville de Paris', a favourite of mine because it is in flower through the whole summer, and the flower heads, a salmon pink with a touch of red, stand up proudly. Then include scented geraniums to pinch as you pass.

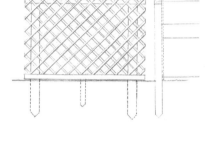

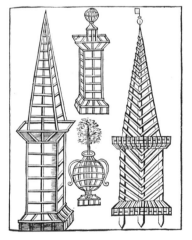

Top: **John Rea's 'Lattice frame' to go round the outer edge of the flower borders, taken from a measured drawing by Peter Goodchild.** *Bottom:* **Trellis-work pyramids and obelisks from J. van der Groen's book on gardening in the Low Countries,** *Le Jardinier du Pays-Bas* **(1681).**

Our verandah pots are smaller larger and important and sometimes I am amazed by how many plants can fit into them. As their centrepiece they each have a two-year-old ivy leaf geranium, one which has a stout stem and can cope with the wind if properly staked. Our choice is a double mauve variety which again is a generous flowerer. The best plants you have should go round these, but they must blend in colour.

There are more barrels round the kitchen-garden door. One has permanent shrubs in it, a *Fremontidendron californicum* surrounded by golden lonicera which is kept clipped and low. Two others have winter and summer changes: for winter, daffodils are used with wallflowers and hyacinths and in summer there will be white Paris daisies which flower non-stop. However, the most important pots are those with herbs, French tarragon and basil.

The pots on the steps into the house are treated as flower arrangements and are moved around to look their best. We have been collecting as many different geraniums as possible, especially those with soft colours and scented leaves.

If you live as we do with a lime soil the best way to grow lilies is in pots. We order a few each year and they stand where we sit in the evening for their scent. Other plants for this same purpose are fuchsias. With their long-flowering period they make a handsome contribution to the terrace or patio garden. An idea which I have seen recently and looked very good was box balls in pretty stone vases along a very windy terrace.

I have left the grand Versailles tubs until last as there are relatively few places where they look right. Outside a large house, on the driveway or in a formal parterre or wide terrace, they fit the situation. Small reproductions can suit formal town gardens. The proportion of the plant used must be right and there is no reason to think that the conventional bay trees clipped into a pyramid or ball, or even an orange or lemon tree are the only suitable subjects. Other shrubs which you could choose from are standard Portugal laurels (*Prunus lusitanicus*), standard gooseberries, *Viburnum opulus*, *Hydrangea paniculata*, *Euonymus fortunei*. You could experiment with any other small tree or shrub which clips well and makes a firm head—not forgetting the useful hollies.

Trellis Work

Trellis work, or treillage, is an attractive and versatile addition to almost any garden. It is not costly, nor too time-consuming to put up. It is decorative, can be used as a firm support for climbing plants or for training espaliers and cordons, and makes an immediate barrier so that you can make an instant secret garden, quiet arbour or archway.

Trellis work is so easy and simple to make that it has been a constant feature in gardens for centuries. We find it depicted in the wall-paintings taken from Pompeii in the Naples museum, in medieval manuscripts and many of the early gardening books.

In England, Thomas Hill uses a low trellis-work fence, very simply constructed round the inside portion of his small square garden of 1568. John Rea in *Flora, Ceres and Pomona* (1665 and 1676) describes how to make a 'Lattice Frame' to go around the outer edge of the flower borders. The posts should be 5 in (35 cm) square and stand about 4 ft (120 cm) out of the ground, then 'Nail good well-prepared Laths sloping, six inches assunder, both ways Chequer-wise, as every Joyner knows how'.

At the time Rea was writing, J. van der Groen was making drawings of trellis work obelisks, archways, tunnels and pavilions. These appeared in the French translation of his book on gardening in the Low Countries, and the more elaborate drawings indicate how complicated trellis work was becoming, as well as suggesting a strong French appetite for this sort of decoration. D'Argenville's *The Theory and Practice of Gardening* (1709) contains a chapter devoted to very ambitious porticoes, bowers and cabinets of lattice work —all so costly and elaborate, as the text says, that only princes and ministers of state could afford to have them built. Amusing and decorative though they are, the English and Dutch ideas are much more appropriate for a private garden today.

Recently-made trellis-work pyramids designed by the Rev. Henry Thorold for supporting clematis in his borders at Marston Hall, Lincolnshire.

A white-painted verandah along the side of the house at Abbots Ripton Hall, Cambridgeshire. The trellis work in the background creates a pretty *trompe l'oeil* effect.

A white-painted verandah along the side of the house at Abbots Ripton Hall, Cambridgeshire. The trellis work in the background creates a pretty *trompe l'oeil* effect.

'Even as the garden of Pleasure is to be set about with arbours, covered with jessamine, musk roses, myrtle trees, bay trees, woodbind, vines, sweet bryer and other rare things, even so shall the kitchen garden be set with Turrets of lattice fashion, covered over with Bourdeaux vines, or with the best sete of vines that are to be got in the country.'

The Countrie Farme, trans., GERVASE MARKHAM, 1616.

PRACTICAL TRELLIS WORK

There are many practical ways to use trellis-work in your garden today. In a small garden or tiny courtyard which is surrounded by walls it can be devised to create a *trompe l'oeil* effect. Make two panels of trellis and attach these to the wall, leaving enough space between them for a wooden archway. Inside this you could have either a mirror or painting of a path going on through the garden. Upright evergreens such as Irish junipers or yews, planted or in pot, either side of your 'archway' would help the illusion.

A long thin garden might be divided into two sections by trellis work with two or three openings, covered with climbers, honeysuckles, sweet peas, climbing roses or even runner beans.

In a new garden with no existing tall features or trees trellis work may be built to create instant height and shelter round your sitting-out place or as a screen to hide compost bins and other unattractive necessities. Treat the trellis as a non-permanent thing and plant either a hedge or some evergreen shrubs in front, ready to take over the screening job when the trellis has seen better days.

If you are planning a rose garden, arches and a surround made of trellis will provide a feeling of enclosure and also a useful means of support for your climbing roses. What better way to make a central feature than with a trellis work open arbour? This feature would fit appropriately into your vegetable garden covering it with vines, the golden hop, sweet peas or some of the decorative climbing beans.

One thought in the garden usually leads to another and the moment you start to be creative about features you will have brilliant ideas of your own and see things in other people's gardens which you can adapt. This is why it is almost essential to keep a garden note-book—put things down so you do not forget them. A recent winter visit to a garden designed in part by Sir Edwin Lutyens revealed that a stone wall near the house was covered with diamond-shaped lattice work, each strip at least a foot apart. This is used for training and tying in the climbers and also for helping the other shrubs to keep a firm association with the wall. On summer visits I had been unaware of this lattice.

A final thought. If you have a potting shed or garage which is unattractive but essential, it is quicker and easier to buy some of those ready-made trellis panels you see in garden centres and cover the walls with it, providing a support for clematis, roses, honeysuckle, annual climbers, in fact any plant which is non-clinging and requires encouragement.

One of the rose-covered trellis-work arbours in the *potager* at Villandry.

Sundials

Statues and obelisks, bee skips and bird tables may stand in the shadow of your trees or inside a niche in your wall or yew hedge, but your sundial must have a position where the sun will shine on it every hour of the day. Put it in the middle of your herb garden, parterre or rose garden. If you have not one of these, then make it a focal point or centre-piece on your lawn, or at the end of the garden where you must walk to when your watch has stopped.

In the sixteenth century, when Shakespeare wrote, 'Methinks it were a happy life, / To carve out dials quaintly point by point', it was important for the housewife to have a sundial to turn to in order to discover the hour, for quite probably she would not own a watch. I often think that this lack of clocks was the magical part of life, helping to keep time at bay and curbing man from fitting too much into it. But with our accurate digital watches and chiming clocks, the stone sundial has become more of an ornament than a necessity in our gardens. Our's, beside the knot garden, is sadly lacking in numerals which have long since become indistinct, although the essential gnomon is still there to cast its shadow.

If you are fortunate enough to find an old sundial, site it well. If it has lost its true face then do not give it a brand new one, it is much more in keeping to work out where the hours should be and find a stone carver who will decorate it for you.

One temptation is to plant thymes, lavender or rosemary round your sundial to set it off. If you do this, then remember to leave a pathway, or even two, leading right up to it, or your plants will be trampled. Camomile should do well there, for as Shakespeare knew, the more it is trodden on the more it will flourish.

There are plenty of trite, old-fashioned mottoes which have been used to remind us of the flight of time. If you wish to add one which, in spite of its age might be original, here are three suggestions:
Diogenes: 'Nothing costs us so dear as a waste of time.'
Emerson: 'Life is so short that there is always time for courtesy.' Goethe: 'We always have time enough, if we will but use it right.'
To select the best, I must turn to my old friend, William Lawson, the clergyman gardener in the seventeenth century and follow his philosophy: 'What joy may you have, that you living to such an age, shall see the blessing of God on your labour.'

READING LIST

Sixteenth and Seventeenth Centuries

Austin, Ralph *A Treatise of Fruit Trees*, 1653
Bacon, Francis *Essay 'Of Gardens'*, n.d.
Colonna, Francesco *Hypnerotomachia Poliphili*, 1499
The Strife of Love in a Dream, 1592
The Dream of Poliphilus, 1888
Androuet du Cerceau, Jacques *Les Plus Excellents Bastiments de France*, 1578-79
Blake, Stephen *The Complete Gardener's Practice*, 1664
Boyceau de la Baraudiere, Jacques *Traite du Jardinage*, 1638
Columella *On Agriculture*, trans. H.C.Ash, 1941-55
Cato and Varro *On Agriculture*, trans. H.C.Ash and W.D. Hooper, 1955
Evelyn, John *A Discourse of Sallets*, 1699
Evelyn John *Kalendarium Hortense*, 1676
Gardiner, Richard *Profitable Instructions for the Manuring, Sowing, Planting of Kitchen Gardens*, 1599
Gilbert, Samuel *The Florist's Vade-mecum*, 1682
Hill, Thomas *The Proffitable Arte of Gardening, now the third time set forth*, 1568
Hill, Thomas (under the pseudonym Didymus Mountaine), *The Gardener's Labyrinth*, 1577
Lawson, William *The Country House-wife's Garden*, 1617
Lawson, William *A New Orchard and Garden*, 1618
Markham, Gervase *The Countrie Farme*, 1616, trans. from the French
Meager, Leonard *The New Arte of Gardening*, 1697
Parkinson, John *Paradisi in Sole Paradisus Terrestris*, 1629
Rea, John *Flora Ceres and Pomona*, 2nd Ed., 1676
Strabo, Walafrid *Hortulus*, tenth-century poem, trans. by Raef Payne, 1966
Worlidge, John *Systema Horti-culturae; or the Art of Gardening*, 1677
Vries, Jan Vredman de *Hortorum Viridariorumque Elegantes*, 1583

Eighteenth Century

Bradley, Richard *The Gentleman and Gardener's Kalender*, 1718
Chambers, Sir William *A Dissertation on Oriental Gardening*, 1772
Hanbury, William *A Complete Body of Planting and Gardening*, 1770 and 1771
James, John *The Theory and Practice of Gardening*, 1712
Langley, Batty *New Principles of Gardening*, 1728
London, George and Wise, Henry *The Retir'd Gard'ner*, 2 vols., 1706
Repton, Humphry *Observations on the Theory and Practice of Landscape Gardening*, 1803
Switzer, Stephen *Ichnographia Rustica; or, the nobleman's, gentleman's and gardner's recreation*, 3 vols. 1718
Whateley, Thomas *Observations on Modern Gardening*, 1770

Nineteenth Century

Amherst, Alicia *A History of Gardening in England*, 1896
Blomfield, Reginald and Thomas, Inigo *The Formal Garden in England*, 1892
Bright, Henry *The English Flower Garden*, 1881
Fleming, John *Spring and Winter Flower Gardening as practised at Cliveden*, 1870
Hibberd, Shirley *Rustic Adornments for Homes of Taste*, 1870
Gertrude Jekyll: all her books.
Kemp, Edward *How to Lay Out the Garden*, 3rd ed., 1864
Loudon, John *Encyclopaedia of Gardening*, 1832
Loudon, Jane *The Ladies's Magazine of Gardening*, 1842
M'Intosh, Charles *The Flower Garden*, 1839
Papworth, J.B. *Ornamental Gardening*, 1823
Robinson, William *The English Flower Garden*, 1883
Robinson, William *The Wild Garden*, 1894

ACKNOWLEDGEMENTS

t = top, b = bottom, a = above, bl = below, l = left, r = right.

Edwin Smith: pp.9 tr, 14 t, 95, 98 b, 115 b, 139 tl, 150, 155. *Courtauld Institute of Art*: 10. *Country Life*: 11, 65 t and b, 99 r, 128 tl. *Pamla Toler*: 13 t, 81, 84 t, 101 b, 115 tr, 117 tl, 142. *Jerry Harpur*: 13 b, 105, 151 tl and r. *Rosemary Verey*: 14 b, 22 t, 25, 28 t, 32, 36, 37 a, 38, 41 a, 43, 51 b, 59, 70 t and b, 79 b, 97, 98 t, 107, 108, 111 b, 137 b, 139 tr, 153. *Cressida Pemberton Piggott*: 15, 23, 26, 28 b, 29 r, 33, 82, 86, 92, 101 t. *A-Z Collection*: 16 tr, 17, 29 l, 58 t and b, 67 t and b, 78, 79 t, 80, 83, 85, 89, 91, 109 b, 118, 119, 127 b, 134 t and br, 135 tl and b. *Bridgeman Art Library*: 18 and 145 t (*with the Trustees of the British Library*), 34, 55 (*with the Christopher Wood Gallery*). *George Wright*: 27, 109 t. *Pierpont Morgan Library, New York*: 28 tl. *Ian Cameron*: 31, 35, 37, 40 b, 42 b, 66, 106, 110 b, 111 t, 117 b, 123, 148. *Bodleian Library, Oxford*: 46. *Gary Rogers*: 39, 40 a. *Angelo Hornak*: 47, cover. *Marina Schinz*: 50 tl. *Peter Haydon*: 50 br, 99 l, 113 r, 114, 115 tl, 146, 154. *D.Neale*: 51 tl. *National Monuments Record*: 54, 127 t. *R.C. Balfour*: 56. *Metropolitan Museum of Art, New York, Gift of John T. Rockefeller Jr., The Cloisters Collection, 1937*: 75. *Alan Gore*: 41 b, 84 b, 122. *French Government Tourist Office*: 96, 113 l, 151 b. *Ladew Topiary Gardens Foundation*: 103. *Derry Moore*: 117 b. *Valerie Finnis*: 128 tr, 129. *Joe Elliott*: 130, 131. *Penny Strange*: 132. *Francis Cabot*: 135 tr, 137 t and bl. *Charles Verey*: 149 b.